Woolly Jumper

The *true* story of an eccentric
Irish Water Spaniel

by
Dennis McCarthy M.B.E.

Illustrated by
Pete Dredge

Books by Dennis McCarthy include:
The Afghan Hound
The Cocker Spaniel
Local Boy Makes Good
B.B.C. Quiz Book
Leo C. Wilson on dogs
(Co-edited with Kristina Husberg)

Printed by Rainbow Press, Broadway House, Brook Street, Sutton-in-Ashfield, Notts. NG17 1AL. Telephone 0623 550489.

I S B N 0 9518266 1 1

Preface

Woolly Jumper was an eccentric Irish Water Spaniel. She was rather special and I am not sure, as I start to write this account of her life, that I can do justice to her. For ten years she was very much part of our family and gave a great deal of affection and support. All dogs are special in their own way and they all have their own individual personalities – but Woolly Jumper was something else. Her personality was unlike any dog we ever owned. She was a clown, a guard, a companion and a matriarchal figure totally in charge of her own family community.

Do we miss her? Now, that's where words do fail. Years after her passing we still think of her and her presence is still with us.

This book is a tribute to a pedigree dog who never won a prize at a Championship dog show but was a Champion character to everyone who knew her.

CONTENTS

CHAPTER ONE

INTRODUCTION

The story really begins on October 16th 1956. That's when "Gay Princess of Paree" was born. She was a black Miniature Poodle and we called her Dumpy. I bought her when she was three months old for entirely the wrong reason. I was producing and appearing in a play staged by an amateur dramatic society. It was called "On Monday Next" and it was a very funny comedy. One of the female characters carried a tiny Poodle puppy with her wherever she went on stage. I bought Dumpy to play the part.

When the play was over Dumpy went to live with my in-laws and she led a happy life until she was an old lady.

"Fowey" then came into our lives. I bought her for three guineas (£3.15) and this time for the right reason. We wanted a dog.

Fowey was a Labrador cross terrier of some sort. She was born in August 1957 and she was one of the most loyal and loving dogs I ever owned. She had a degree of obedience but she also had a will of her own. She didn't like being restricted by a dog lead and liked to be free.

She was a bit of a devil when she was in season and ready for mating. We had to watch her very carefully and once she "befriended" a large black dog and went off for a couple of days while we were searching

1

everywhere for her. We found them four miles away living in sin on a traffic island in a residential area of Nottingham, known as 'The Park'. We had no problem getting the resulting litter of puppies good homes. Fowey's fame had spread far and wide. She appeared on stage as a character in a play I wrote which received a lot of newspaper publicity.

An example of Fowey's loyalty was shown when I had quite a serious accident. I was selling washing machines in Norfolk and I used to arrive in the Kings Lynn area at about 6 o'clock in the evening for various pre-arranged appointments until around midnight with my van full of machines. I always travelled in the large van with Fowey and an Afghan called Zaza – I'll tell you about her later.

Around 2 a.m. one morning I was travelling through Boston in Lincolnshire on my way home to Nottingham and I fell asleep at the wheel. I woke up with the van bumping along the grass at the side of the road and I vaguely remember sliding down a dyke heading for a tree. The van was a write-off.

The front passenger seat where Fowey and Zaza had been curled up together was pierced by the shattered windscreen of the van.

A lorry driver found me crawling in the middle of the A17 road and by my side was Fowey. There was no sign of Zaza. An ambulance took me to Boston hospital and Fowey travelled with me. I was admitted to hospital and Fowey was taken to a local Vet's kennels.

I was distraught over Zaza's disappearance but the next day the hospital authorities reluctantly let me go to the scene of the accident in a police car because a very strange and savage looking dog was preventing the police towing away the mangled wreck of my van. We sped to the scene and there was Zaza guarding the van. No amount of persuasion by the police could get her to move. I opened the door of the police car and gently called "Zaza" – she heard me and bounded over to the car, leapt in, and cried for ten minutes. I have never known a dog behave in this way.

In the end all was well. Zaza and Fowey were taken back home and I was discharged from the hospital, bruised, but with no real injury.

Fowey was a delight and when my daughter, Karen, was born she was guarded day and night by Fowey who rarely left her side. Fowey died at the age of 14 in the arms of my wife, Marjorie.

Fowey was three years old when the Afghan Hounds came along. The first was Zaza, a very beautiful black faced golden Afghan. I bought her for 15 guineas from a very famous dog breeder, Eileen Snelling.

Zaza was ten weeks old when I first saw her and I wonder, even now, why Eileen ever sold her to me. My first comment was – "She doesn't look much like an Afghan". She was a great Afghan Hound and became a Champion in the show ring.

I next bought Gina, a black and tan Afghan who was a great character; then I acquired Zoe, a red Afghan who never really settled down with us.

Zaza was about two years old when she had a litter of puppies and we kept a large golden dog and named him Sultan. He was a magnificent specimen and did quite well in the show ring, though he never became a Champion like his mother. He was a great pal and there was a special relationship between us.

Gina's first pregnancy produced problems and we knew all was not well. A Veterinary examination revealed one puppy. "It's enormous" said the Vet, "She won't be able to have it normally, it's probably a monster. We'll take it away in a couple of days time".

Gina defied the Vet and had the puppy quite normally. It was black and silver and we called it Tara, and Tara became a notable Champion and is still remembered by some today. She was the biggest clown I ever knew and her reputation in the show ring was considerable. I never knew what she would do. We would get visitors from the Continent and America and Australia who would suddenly descend on the kennel, often without prior warning, to see Tara. She used to jump on a low wall and pose for photographs. Afghan Hounds are supposed to be dignified and aloof. Tara could be just that, when she wanted, or she could act the clown. She would throw her head back and open her mouth and appear to laugh. She had tan markings about her eyes and she could look very fierce. I think she knew this and she would sometimes dash up to strangers in a very threatening way, stop short and laugh her head off at their reaction. What a character!

We bred more Afghans and they did very well in the show ring. Then along came "Bonny" – her registered name was Tzara of Pooghan. Her father was a handsome black and silver dog called Ashley and her mother was a very lovely golden Afghan called Arafekh – named after an Egyptian Mummy in a Derby museum. Ashley was Champion Tara's son and Arafekh was Champion Zaza's daughter, so the pedigree was superb. Very often when two Afghans get together it all looks great on paper but the result is disappointing. Not this time. It was a perfect match and Bonny looked good from the very beginning. In fact, we filmed her when she was twenty minutes old and we kept on filming her until she was about eight years. The result was a remarkable film called "Born to be a Champion".

Bonny did well in the show ring from the start of her show career. She

3

won Best Puppy and Best in Show when she was just six months old, at her very first show. And she kept on winning. It takes the winning of three Challenge Certificates to gain the title of 'Champion'. Bonny won 21 Certificates and over 20 reserve Certificates, all under different judges. I believe she still holds the record for winning so much under different judges.

We took her to Ireland, where she was a sensation. At her first show in Dublin the other Afghan exhibitors heard about her attendance and met us at the entrance to the show. They told us we shouldn't go on the benches but go straight to the ringside. They had prepared a place for her and put down a large travelling rug for her to lie on. She won the Green Star (the Irish Certificate). The Judge was an American lady – we didn't know her – and I think if she had given the main award to any other dog the spectators would have lynched her.

Bonny visited Ireland five times and won the Green Star every time. It made her an International Champion and she was fêted throughout the dog world. She died at the age of nine with a brain tumour and is buried at Bingham, in Nottinghamshire, by the side of Buggins Cottage, where we now live.

Her death knocked the stuffing out of us and we went to very few dog shows after she died. With Bonny we could go to any dog show of any size and know that we had a chance of winning the top prize. After she had gone there was not much incentive to attend shows with the Afghans.

Along the way I have missed quite a number of notable Afghans in our kennels. And my wife, Marjorie, had some great Poodles. Marvellous characters that we remember still with a great deal of affection long after their passing.

Our children grew up with the dogs and my daughter, Karen, co-owned a quite outstanding black Miniature Poodle Champion, called Zardin.

Marjorie had some lovely white Poodles and did a lot of winning. They glistened in the show ring and were always beautifully presented. She had a great black Poodle called Nicholas. Nick lived in the house with a gorgeous platinum Afghan called Laura. Nick died at the age of $17^1/2$ years. He won a Certificate and we teased the whole of the dog world by entering him at Crufts at the age of 17. At that time Crufts had a restricted entry and you had to be a top current winner or have a Certificate to be allowed to enter.

Nick was qualified – so we entered him. His entry caused quite a stir among the dog fraternity and in the newspapers. There never was a chance of him going to Crufts because by then he was very wobbly on his legs and he was blind. His blindness didn't bother him at all and the other kennel dogs were very kind to him. And, of course, we loved Nick dearly.

When I bought Fowey I lived with my wife and two children, Karen and Owen, at Carlton in Nottingham, in a detached house on the top of a steep hill surrounded by an estate of houses. It was not suitable for a kennel of dogs at all and we had a lot of trouble with neighbours. I think their complaints were probably justified. The dogs howled, sometimes in the middle of the night, and they would occasionally escape into nearby gardens and dig holes in lawns.

Zoe, the Afghan, once got out and came back an hour later carrying in her mouth a very large meat joint that was obviously someone's Sunday dinner.

I don't know how I managed to care for and feed the dogs. I had difficulty in earning enough money to feed my family. My wife divorced me and I entered one of the saddest periods of my life. My dogs kept me sane. Their friendship meant a great deal to me. It's true that I often thought of ending everything and when I had the accident in the van on the Boston road, several friends thought I had deliberately crashed to kill myself. That isn't true.

Eventually things sorted themselves out and I moved to Wilford near Nottingham, in an old 15th century farm house which I rented for £3 per week. The house I owned with my wife at Carlton had a £10 a month mortgage. I fell behind with the payments and the Church of England Building Society snatched the house from me in a most un-Christian like way and I was out on the streets. I found Riverbank Farm at Wilford and I was happy there for nearly 14 years.

Most of the Afghan Hounds were born at Wilford and we also had cats, geese, Muscovy ducks and peacocks. The peacocks were fairly disastrous and tended to perch right on top of the farmhouse near to the chimney pots and no amount of coaxing would get them down. They called very loudly at dawn and what with the cackling geese, the honking peacocks and the howling dogs we were soon in trouble again with the neighbours. We got blamed for every noisy dog in a radius of two miles and many of the complaints were unjustified. The neighbours called in the police to check the noise levels but the police told me that their checks proved the complaints unfounded. The police also told me that if I moved out of Riverbank Farm the whole neighbourhood would be done over by villains. Sure enough, when we did eventually move the burglars moved in.

Riverbank Farm had no land with it, just a small square area surrounded by stables. We made these into kennels but to try and cut down the noise and howling we moved the dogs into a cellar dairy in the house where they were a little more comfortable and quieter.

The landlord doubled the rent to £6 a week – I married Marjorie – two years later our daughter, Tara, was born and we moved to Bingham right on the Roman Fosse Road in a small cottage which first appeared on the map in 1690. The cottage was far too small for us. Riverbank Farm had 5 bedrooms. Buggins Cottage, Bingham, had just one bedroom that someone sometime had divided into two.

It was a long way away from any other human habitation and was, and is, ideal for the dogs. Not for the first time we thought more of the dogs than our own comfort. We had a large long dog run, well fenced, and built a large brick kennel with two large compartments and a corridor. We also built a dog kitchen with a large sink for bathing the dogs in and next door we built a maternity kennel. In front of this was a large puppy run, well fenced in. For dogs – ideal; for us – very cramped. But we have been very happy at Buggins and in the summer it can be peaceful and beautiful. We adapted to the cramped conditions and we now love it at Buggins and don't really ever want to move again.

I never could manage money and got into terrible financial difficulties at Carlton, where, as I have explained, I lost the house. We didn't fare much better at Riverbank Farm, and with a £3 a week rent I often got into arrears.

I was in danger at Riverbank Farm of becoming almost a hermit. My painting and decorating business had collapsed; my 12 month stint unsuccessfully selling washing machines was disastrous. My boss said I thought too much of the customer and not enough of the Company. This type of selling is fairly high pressure and I had qualms about selling washing machines to old ladies who really couldn't manage them properly and families who really couldn't afford to keep up the payments.

We started up a dog tripe business that was very successful for about six weeks and then we lost our supply of tripe, so that was the end of that. I fell into a depression and stayed in the house.

BBC Local Radio started in Nottingham in 1968 and I thought I would be a natural gift for radio. I don't know why. Apart from two brief appearances on Television with my Afghans I had no broadcasting experience at all. Mind you, very few people in Local Radio had much experience of broadcasting at that time. I applied for a job with BBC

Radio Nottingham and I received the fastest rejection slip ever sent to anyone. My educational qualifications were practically nil. I had done well at school but it had been an Elementary school – a type of education so humble that it no longer exists.

I persevered with the BBC and persuaded them to let me broadcast a report about Crufts and local dog exhibitors. It went down very well and they promised to pay me £1. The following week I reported on local dog breeders exporting dogs to many parts of the world. That went down well again and I was promised another £1.

For ten weeks I reported on local dogs and was promised £1 each time but so far had received nothing. By this time I couldn't afford the bus fare into the City centre to make the broadcasts and I took my courage in both hands and asked the Programme Organiser if there was a chance of getting the £10 the BBC now owed me. They paid me and I bought a modern radio set for £8, which meant I could now hear the Local Radio broadcasts.

I then decided to offer an interview about brewery horses. This was accepted and I was paid £2. By then a couple of producers had spotted my potential and I was given a shared desk in an office and I started my broadcasting career.

Twelve months later I was doing 20 interviews a week, had a 15 minute programme about dogs – the first in this country; a 30 minute chat show and I was a regular contributor to a dozen other programmes every week. Television soon followed and eventually I hosted the Crufts Television programmes for six years and was seen in many different countries. I had, by then, started judging dog shows and gave Certificates in this country as well as Norway, Sweden, Finland, Belgium and Ireland.

I still can't manage money but there is now a safe roof over our heads and there is food on the table and a fire in the hearth. Everything is now paid for, I don't owe anyone anything. All thanks to my dogs giving me an introduction to the BBC. I give all this background to my start in dogs and the setting up of my kennels to give you an insight into the environment into which came Woolly Jumper.

I once read a book about dogs in which it was stated that the Irish Water Spaniel is the world's most intelligent breed of dog. I don't know where the writer got this piece of information. I don't think he or she ever owned an Irish Water Spaniel but having read this, I always wanted to own one.

Marjorie, of course, shared my love of dogs but was always wary of me adding to our growing menagerie.

7

We had a lot of dogs and a couple of lovely cats by this time and they took a lot of her time. I persuaded her that we should really go into another group of dogs. We had Poodles which were in the Utility group; we had Afghans which were in the Hound group; we should now look to the Gundog group and an Irish Water Spaniel. And with it being "The World's most intelligent dog" it would be no trouble to us. Its intelligence would be appreciated in the house and it would virtually take care of itself. In addition, by then I was becoming a much sought after judge of dogs of all breeds and I felt we ought to get to know more intimately another breed totally different from our existing collection of dogs.

We examined all the literature about Irish Water Spaniels. There isn't a great deal.

To say that the Irish Water Spaniel appeared as a distinct breed just over a hundred years ago, it is quite surprising that little is known about its early beginnings. It seems to have made its first appearance around 1880 or just a little before. One of the first exhibitors and the man who probably had most to do with the 'creation' of the breed was a Mr. McCarthy. The thought that one of my ancestors actually started up the Irish Water Spaniel might well have encouraged me to own one.

It was probably a cross between the Standard Poodle and the Irish Setter. In Ireland they seem to like the colour red. They even have red lemonade which I was introduced to on one of my visits to the country. At the end of the 19th century they had a Red Setter, Red Spaniel, Red Terrier, Red Wolfhound and a Red Horse. Strictly speaking the Irish Water Spaniel's colour is known as a rich dark liver.

The breed was developed to become a water retriever but it could do so many different jobs and it was useful for the sportsman of limited means who hadn't the accommodation for a team of dogs. It could do the duties of a Pointer, Setter, Retriever and Spaniel. So you have the picture of a Gundog, a sporting dog that would be greatly treasured by its owner. Of course, I have no interest in shooting game or anything else so I knew when we thought of getting an Irish Water Spaniel I would not exercise its talents with the gun.

I am always interested in the character of a dog and in all the descriptions of the Irish Water Spaniel the experts talk about the loyalty and the deep affectionate nature. It's a very distinct breed and once you know what it is you never forget it. A lot of people ask – "Is it a Standard Poodle?" They can be forgiven because there is obviously Poodle in its make-up.

Before we bought Woolly we examined carefully the Breed Standard of the Irish Water Spaniel. It's to be smart, upstanding, strongly built and compact. The temperament should include a sense of humour, the eyes intelligent and alert; the ears are long, oval shaped, the jaw is strong; it has a powerful arched neck, deep chest, broad back, large feet with hair over and between the toes. The tail is fairly short, straight, thick at the root and tapering to a fine point, close curls of hair at the root but the rest of the tail is bare. When the dog moves it has a rolling gait. The coat consists of tight ringlets or curls and the hair has a natural oiliness, and there's a top-knot of curly hair on the head. The colour is a rich dark liver with a purplish tint or bloom.

There you have the official description of the Irish Water Spaniel and we had all that in mind when we were looking for a puppy. Needless to say, Woolly didn't fit the description and when we first saw her she could have been any one of a dozen breeds.

The Irish Water Spaniel is a fairly rare breed of dog and there are not many puppies bred each year compared with more popular breeds. We scanned the advertisements in the dog magazines but there was no sign of any Irish Water Spaniels. One Saturday morning we were reading the magazines and saw a litter advertised in Leicester, which was only about half an hour away from Buggins Cottage. We telephoned about the puppies and said we would call to see them and off we went.

We arrived and were shown into a large kitchen. The eight week old puppies were all under a table and most of them didn't want to know us. That's fairly standard with most puppies. One came out to us wagging its tail and grinning. It was very friendly – far more than its brothers and sisters.

We were told that the Irish Water Spaniel Committee had seen the puppies and declared them all to be of show quality. Since the Irish Water Spaniel Committee probably came from the four corners of the country I found it strange that they should all descend on this Leicester household to look at baby puppies and have such faith in their development.

They were small, not fully developed in shape, size, coat or any of the other desired points. I think anyone who promises anything with such babies is risking their judgement and expertise.

We straight away said she looked like a Woolly Jumper and that name stuck. She was friendly, bold, healthy and you really can't expect anything else of an 8 week old puppy of any breed. Marjorie and Tara looked at me – but we didn't have to discuss anything, we were hooked. I was kneeling on the floor and Woolly came up to me and snuggled against me. She knew from an early age how to enter the hearts of people.

9

We paid £80 – it was a fair amount of money at the time, we were given a pedigree which meant very little to us except it did look a bit of a jumble with no positive line breeding, and we took Woolly home with us.

She came in the house a little hesitantly, we introduced her to Jim, a large half-Persian cat whom we had bought with the house from the previous owner. Jim spat at Woolly but not with too much venom because he had learned to put up with the dogs by now.

Woolly found a rubber ball belonging to Jim and carried it a little way up the garden path and then brought it back to me. She couldn't have done anything better to please me. We had about twenty dogs – Poodles and Afghans – and I had always wanted to play ball with a dog. The idea being to throw a ball some distance and the dog to dutifully bring it back. None of our other dogs had ever done that.

If you threw a ball with an Afghan it would chase it, toss it in the air and then eat it. If you threw a ball to any of the Poodles they would chase it, throw it around a little and soon get disinterested. They wouldn't bring it back. It sounds so simple but we were thrilled.

I threw the ball again. This time Woolly brought back an apple. Here was a dog that was different. Time was to prove that she was not just different – she was **very** different. In her behaviour, her temperament, her moods and her actions. That first day with Woolly was a joy – there was a lot more to come.

CHAPTER
TWO

WOOLLY AND FRIENDS

We decided to call her Woolly Jumper from the very first time we saw her but when we got home our first task was to register her at the Kennel Club. Our kennel name is Pooghan – made up from POOdles and AfGHANs and all the dogs we bred had that name attached to them which means a Pooghan registered dog could be traced back to us.

Many dogs have grand sounding names registered at the Kennel Club. One of Marjorie's Poodles was registered as St. Agathes Summer Breeze. His pet name was Simple Simon. And the great International Champion Tzara of Pooghan was always called Bonny. We thought we wouldn't pussyfoot around with Woolly Jumper and we registered her as just that – "Woolly Jumper of Pooghan". Registration number E731039F2; Irish Water Spaniel, Bitch. Date of Birth: 26/4/80. Sire: Fosse Willow; Dam: Rosetyne Mio Mamba. Now she was all official with a registered name at the Kennel Club.

Very often friends would say – "Woolly Jumper's a good name – but what's her registered name?" And we would say – Woolly Jumper, honestly!

When Woolly first came to us most of our dogs lived outside in the purpose built brick kennels. We always intended that Woolly would live in the house with us and a couple of dogs. At that time we had a golden Afghan called Star, two white Poodles named Bumpy and Jolly Boy and our black Poodle, Nicholas – and the two cats, Jim and Vostock. Vostock was a very beautiful Russian Blue, very strange, as all cats are. He thought he was part dog and part parrot and he had a habit of walking up my back and perching on my shoulder. Minnie, our English Toy Terrier also does this.

We had cats when we lived at Riverbank Farm. We had a Lilac pointed Siamese called Prasert, who won a Certificate at a Championship cat show and before that we had a Seal pointed Siamese named Samantha. She never really settled down with the dogs. She was a very independent character and didn't like the dogs sniffing round her. She was a great hunter and would often bring mice into the house dangling from her mouth. She became quite friendly with some people across the road from us and one day she behaved very strangely in the house, yowling and making a fuss of us – and that wasn't the norm for her. We let her out with the dogs and she jumped on the wall, looked at us and yowled. We petted her and I remember she stuck her tail right up in the air, trotted to the gate, looked at us again, jumped over the gate and left home. She never came back to Riverbank Farm and went to live with the couple across the road.

About a week later they came to see us and explained that Samantha had moved in with them, that they loved her and could they pay for her. We said "No!" If Samantha had decided she didn't want anything to do with us – that really was her business. As I say, she was very independent. Strange animals, cats. Samantha lived happily with her adopted family to a great old age.

When we moved to Buggins Cottage we bought Jim with the property. He was very puzzled by all the dogs. He got used to them eventually and rather liked them and would press himself up against them. They accepted Jim and Jim accepted them.

On our very first day at Buggins as we were moving furniture into the cottage Jim was in the kitchen miaowing loudly. We went in the room to find that he had brought into the centre of the floor a pheasant he'd just caught. I think it was Jim's idea of a house warming present.

Jim was always bringing things home; birds, mice, rats, moles. Usually they were very dead and he would put them outside the back door. We learned to gingerly open the back door and look on the doorstep first thing in the morning to see what was there. Jim once brought back a young rabbit. It was alive and we soothed it and released it in the field next door to Buggins.

Sadly, living right on the Roman Fosse road which has fast moving traffic on it all the time, we lost a lot of cats. I could never understand why they ever went on to the road. They had about 40 acres of fields for hunting at the back of Buggins but in the end they were all drawn to the road. We won't have any more cats. They had a great time with us, I think, but the sadness of losing a cat is too much.

This, then, was Woolly's home, with dogs and cats and wildlife all round. Woolly settled down straight away – I think she was always happy at Buggins and she didn't want to settle with anyone else, like that ungrateful Siamese, Samantha.

Woolly liked the cats and we had quite a number. When we lost Vostock, the Russian Blue, I brought home a little kitten that was about to be destroyed. We called her Minnie the Moocher and for many days she was too scared to come down from the upstairs bedroom window sill. Jim was very kind to Minnie the Moocher and one day he brought a live mouse to her feet to play with. There is no greater display of affection by one cat to another.

I remember Woolly had a way of making friends with our cats by sharing their food bowl. They didn't always appreciate Woolly's interest in their food and would sometimes spit at her, but she never retaliated.

Tiger Lily was another rescued kitten and she lived with Jim on top of the refrigerator, well out of the way of the dogs. Woolly was safe with all the cats and kittens but the other dogs – the Poodles particularly, would sometimes chase the cats. They would stop instantly the cat stopped and gave a warning miaow and then raised a paw that was quite threatening to a small Poodle. I can't remember Woolly ever giving chase to any of the cats. She was a great one for live and let live.

Jake was a strange cat. My niece and her husband brought him to us because they couldn't cope with him. He didn't come out of his basket for 24 hours and he growled at us when we approached him. We put his basket with him inside in the conservatory and left him to it. Our experience has been with both cats and dogs that you can't force them to associate with you – eventually they will come around. It's always worked.

We were leaving food and drink near Jake's basket and he came out in his own time to eat and drink. But one morning we came down to find Jake gone. There was always an open window in the conservatory and Jake had found it. We were very upset. He was over a hundred miles from his previous home and we had no idea where he would go. He

could also be injured on the road and he might be lying in a hedge bottom somewhere.

At that time Tara was in the Brownies and they met once a week at the RAF camp at Newton, which was literally across the road from Buggins. Marjorie took Tara to the camp by car because it was about a mile to the camp entrance. Shortly after Jake disappeared, Marjorie was at the RAF camp and saw a cat in the distance – it looked like Jake but she couldn't get near enough to identify it properly.

She had a word with the Padre and he said, yes, a stray black and white cat had turned up at the camp and was living in the Officers' Mess. Trust Jake to pull rank. It was Jake. The officers locked him in a store room and called Marjorie over. Jake was pleased to see a familiar face and gladly came back to Buggins.

Jake was a changed cat. No more spitting and growling or threatening paw with nails showing. He came into the cottage and settled down as one of us. I always reckoned there was a special affinity between Woolly and Jake. You see, Jake was a clever cat and was able to open the fridge door. I don't know how he did it to this day. But he did. And he and Woolly would raid the fridge for any tasty morsel that might lodge on the shelves. Jake was even cleverer in the garage where we had a large upright freezer. Don't ask me how but he could open the door of that too. We heard a noise in the garage and went to investigate. Jake had got a large piece of frozen meat and was very puzzled as to what to do to it. Woolly didn't even think, she just picked up the meat and took it away with Jake following closely behind.

Smidge and Smudge then came into our lives. They were twin brothers, white with black smudges on them and they were going to be put to sleep – so, I brought them home one evening. Woolly took to them straight away and tended to mother them. We didn't encourage this too much because once, at Riverbank Farm, Champion Tara had mothered a little kitten which curled up with her on the settee. Tara was quite a heavy Afghan and one night she lay on the kitten and squashed it. We didn't want the same thing to happen to Smidge and Smudge and Woolly.

The two kittens were very playful and that's something that Woolly didn't quite understand. Kitten play is something very different to just running for a ball and returning it to your master. In the evenings Woolly would lie in front of the fire and the kittens would get on top of her and slide down her head and they had a peculiar way of showing – well, I think it was affection towards Woolly. They would 'pad' against her –

pressing their paws into her coat and extending their nails. It didn't hurt Woolly at all and I think she was amused by it.

Ginger Crackle was our next cat. He had a virus or something when we first had him and he nearly died. It left him with a nasal problem and he used to snuffle and sneeze – but it wasn't contagious. He was friendly with everyone. Jim didn't like him first of all but then– accepted him. Woolly liked Ginger Crackle because he used to let her share his food bowl. When Ginger Crackle died we decided that we wouldn't have any more cats. Living right up to the main Roman Fosse road was too dangerous, and we couldn't do anything to stop the cats going on the road.

I was very sad to lose Ginger Crackle because I knew he would probably be our last cat and I am very fond of cats. They are obstinate, they are independent, they can be very aloof. But when they love you it is very genuine and they can't control their demonstration of affection. If they are happy and love you – they purr.

They would bite and scratch – but when they purred and rolled over to have a tummy tickled, well, that made up for a lot of their drawbacks. Woolly missed Ginger Crackle when he had gone and she used to sniff the hedge bottoms and search around the freezer in the garage and look into all the little places where Ginger Crackle used to hide and pounce out on Woolly when she passed by.

It was obvious from early days that Woolly was not going to be a show dog. We had great success with our Afghan Hounds in the show–ring and for several years had the top winning Hound in the breed and we aimed for a high standard when we took a dog into the show–ring. Woolly was too tall by inches, her curly coat wasn't tight enough and she didn't really relate to the breed standard of points for the Irish Water Spaniel. She had a good head and a good tail – but you can't take just a head and a tail into the show–ring. There has to be something worthwhile in between.

We didn't mind too much because once we knew she was no good for the show-ring she was one of us and nothing – but nothing – would make us part with her.

We always had at least one Afghan in the house. After Star died, Laura took her place in the house. She came inside just to recuperate from a major operation which had taken hours to perform. Laura was a lovely blonde Afghan and Woolly got on with her very well. Laura was very loving towards us but very aloof and distant with other humans and dogs.

The rest of the Afghans were outside, housed in their kennel, which was very well built – the insulated breeze blocks made it warm in the winter and cool in summer. They had a long dog run, 140 feet by 18 feet, with a 2 metre high strong wire mesh fencing all around. Most of the twenty Afghans we had outside at that time would have a good gallop around the dog run first thing in the morning. We had more safety precautions in case they ever got out of the dog run. They would have got into the garden which, in turn, had another 2 metre fencing built all around. And to get out of that they would have to go through three gates. We knew that if any dog got on to the road they would be killed.

Woolly had the freedom of the house and garden but she was always quite keen to go into the more restricted area of the dog run. When we let her through their gate the Afghans would all rush up to her to inspect her. It would have been daunting to any other dog to have 20 huge Afghans bounding towards them – but not Woolly. She stood her ground – and inspected **them**. Her back would bristle and she would draw herself up to her full height – which was considerable – and she would go around 'bossing' them. She soon made them realise she was the master – or mistress.

She wasn't scared of any of them and, strangely, though she was totally different in shape, temperament and personality they took to her and accepted her as 'one of the boys'. Mind you, she could do something that, thank goodness, none of the Afghans could do. When she was tired of being in the dog run with the Afghans she would climb over the fencing. We couldn't understand how she got out with no–one to open the gate and one day we saw her climb slowly but surely up the mesh fencing and down the other side. I remember seeing a group of Afghans watch her accomplish this feat. They were very puzzled but, thank goodness, didn't try to do the same.

One morning in December 1981 Woolly asked to go into the dog run – it was a cold morning and looked as though rain was threatening so we put the dogs into their kennel and closed the door. Woolly wanted to go in with them, so we let her. We then went off into Nottingham where I was involved in a big charity collection outside the City's Council House. It was very successful and with an army of collectors we gathered in something over £50,000 for the Tuberous Sclerosis Association. It was quite an achievement.

After the event we were anxious to get home, we never liked leaving the kennels without anyone there. It was all fairly safe, the kennels were very solid and the three gates and two lots of fencing meant that the whole complex was escape-proof. As we drove up towards Buggins we sensed something was wrong. We saw an Afghan tail wagging above the weeds in the garden. And when we got out of the car we saw twenty Afghans and an Irish Water Spaniel loose in the garden. None of them was missing, luckily, and we opened the gate to their dog run and they all lumbered in. But we couldn't understand how they had got out of their kennel. Both doors to their kennel compartment were still closed.

We went inside to find that there was a window open and they had all climbed through that to get out in the garden. But how? The window was on two latches. We closed the window and Woolly came into the kennel and in front of us moved one latch with her nose and the other latch with her mouth – and the window opened. She'd let all of them loose. After that we put an additional dog–proof latch on all the windows.

After Laura, Huggy Bear came to live in the house with Woolly and the cats. Huggy Bear was a large golden Afghan with a lovely temperament. I never knew him growl in anger. He came into the house because he had a personal problem and had to have his testicles removed. After that operation we knew he posed no problem with Woolly. We all loved Huggy Bear, he was never a nuisance and blended in with the family perfectly. He would clamber on to an armchair near the fire and would happily stay there all day. Woolly loved him, of course, and every morning cleaned out his ears. He did suffer from a wax problem. Woolly couldn't quite understand why he wasn't interested in her sexually – but it was difficult to explain to an Irish Water Spaniel about Huggy Bear's operation and the resulting effect on his sexual interests.

For six years I presented Crufts on BBC Television. I am proud of that part of my career because the programme achieved an audience in this country of 8,500,000 viewers. And, up to the time of writing, that figure has not been reached again since I left the programme. The programme was hard work spread over a four day period working from around 6 a.m. till up to 1 a.m. the following morning. The pressure was considerable and the aim was to produce a high quality programme about dogs of interest to everyone. We made them quite entertaining with dogs and personalities at the world's most famous dog show.

I took Tara with me to help because I did need a lot of assistance. We finished the programme late on Sunday evening and tried to catch a train home straight away. Sometimes we worked so late that we had to stay at an hotel on the Sunday night and travel home by train the next morning.

After one of the Crufts visits Tara rather surprised us by saying she wanted a dog of her own. Since we had over twenty dogs in the kennel at that time and she was fond of all of them we were a bit shaken at her wanting another dog. But she was 13 years old and very sensible about dogs and wouldn't want one as a novelty or as a sudden fancy in a moment of madness. We asked her what she would like. We were sure she would like a big dog. We had some good friends who had an Irish Wolfhound and we knew that Tara liked it a great deal. We already had big Afghans and Woolly was in the 'big' category.

Tara quietly said she wanted an English Toy Terrier. I had judged them with other breeds of dogs at shows but we really didn't know anything about living with them and asked why she wanted a dog of this breed. It turned out that while she was with me at Crufts doing the Television programme she had wandered around the Toy dog benches and had seen the English Toy Terriers and had been taken by them. They seemed intelligent and smart and friendly – and she wanted one.

We looked for an English Toy Terrier puppy and asked around and found out they were fairly rare – not many puppies were bred each year. We were told that we might have to wait up to six months for a bitch and that it might be easier to get a dog. We searched the dog papers and came across an advertisement for a male English Toy Terrier; $4^1/2$ months old; good home essential. I phoned the number quoted and spoke to Richard Haynes. I told him I wanted a good dog and asked him some questions about his puppy. He was in Manchester and we made arrangements for Marjorie and Tara to travel up by train where the puppy would be brought to the station, they would have a good look at him and if they didn't like him – that would be it, no harm done, they would go home without him.

Richard couldn't be at the station so his mother brought the puppy in a basket. There wasn't a great deal of time before the return train to Nottingham and Marjorie and Tara liked what they saw and paid £150 for Hector. They had taken a cat basket with them and Hector was transferred over and had a pleasant train journey back home where he insisted on being taken out of the basket and amused fellow passengers by wagging his tail furiously whenever anyone passed by.

I was asleep on the settee when they arrived home and was awoken by this funny little black and tan puppy walking along the back of the settee and licking my face. He was a charmer, very handsome, his ears were folded down but we knew English Toy Terriers could be like that as puppies. He was so friendly, never stopped wagging his tail and cuddled up close to me on the settee. Now, Hector knew that Tara was his Mum and there has always been a special relationship between them – but he made it obvious that he regarded me as his Dad.

21

I fell in love with the funny little character. I loved his personality, his sense of humour, his playing. Within two days he had a collection of slippers, scraps of paper, half empty toilet rolls, rubber balls and squeaky toys littered all over Buggins Cottage. I had to have an English Toy Terrier for myself.

We scanned the dog papers again and this time I was looking for a bitch. We spread the word round and received a call from Birmingham. There was a bitch available. We took Hector and other members of the family and saw a couple of puppies. One of them was Minnie. She was very small but seemed to have all the essentials and I paid out £150 and found myself the owner of Arzelah Charlock – whom we quickly named Minnie. Hector, incidentally, was paid for by Tara out of her own savings – though I don't think there was much left in the savings account after buying him.

The journey home was interesting. We had with us my son, Digger, his wife, Sue and their year old daughter, Genevieve; The car was quite crowded. Hector sniffed Minnie – Minnie snapped at him and told him to remember his place, and, frankly, she's done that to him ever since. They are inseparable but if he ever gets out of hand she reprimands him.

In the car Minnie curled up with Genevieve and behaved very well. When we got home Minnie settled in straight away. Meanwhile, we wondered how Woolly would react to the two newcomers. She was quite capable of being jealous and the English Toy Terriers were very small. Would she snap at them? She was capable of biting off their heads. How would they react to her? She must have seemed very big to a tiny English Toy Terrier.

They sniffed her – and she sniffed them – and first impressions seemed very good. They played around a lot and she gave a warning growl if they were too boisterous and came too near her den. Minnie and Hector loved squeaky toys and we bought them quite a collection. Woolly liked squeaky toys too and stole quite a number from under the Toy Terriers' noses. But she brought them back to them, usually after she had broken the squeak.

I think Minnie and Hector knew they had come into Woolly's territory. She bossed them a little but they took that well. In her own way Woolly was quite gentle with them.

Hector was a very inquisitive dog and it was quite natural for us to register him at the Kennel Club with the name – "Hector the Inspector of Pooghan". We took him to a dog show because he was a very good specimen, but he didn't like showing, and he didn't like strangers touching him. He had to get to know them first and that wasn't possible at a dog show.

A dog stands on a table and the judge approaches it and looks at the dog's teeth. There's no formal introduction, no time to get used to the judge – and Hector didn't like that at all. Since we've never thought it fair to take a dog to a dog show where the dog didn't feel happy – we decided to scrap the idea of making Hector into a Champion. Minnie was a different kettle of fish. She didn't care who looked at her teeth and thought there was always a possibility that they might have food to give her, so she showed well and at one of her first shows won the reserve Certificate, which was a good win.

Minnie was a good show dog and, in my view, ought to have been a Champion. There were several occasions when she was considerably much better than dogs which beat her for prizes. Unfortunately she had a scrap with another of our dogs called Melody. Minnie came off worst and knocked out two of her front teeth – and that saw the end of her show career.

The origin and history of the English Toy Terrier is shrouded in some mystery, like most breeds. It was bred to be a ratter and came to look something like the present dog around the late 1800s, though something resembling an English Toy Terrier has been documented since 1500. It's a smaller version of the Manchester Terrier who have their ears down – the English Toy Terrier has erect ears when adult, and it's a finer and more elegant dog than the Manchester Terrier. It descended from the old Black and Tan rough haired terrier and there are probably a number of breeds mixed in to give its coat, colour and shape.

It's known to be attractive, affectionate with its family, a game little dog, fearless and loyal – but it tends to attach itself to one person usually. Not many people recognise them in the street and you get comments like: "Is it a Miniature Dobermann?", and someone once told me with great conviction that it was a Tibetan Spaniel. It doesn't look anything like a Tibetan Spaniel and I always gently tell inquirers that it is an English Toy Terrier. Hardly anyone gets it right first time.

To Woolly, the English Toy Terriers were just dogs – rather strange little things in her eyes, I suspect.

Eventually Hector and Minnie mated and a litter of three puppies arrived. There was a small one, a medium sized one and a larger one. Hector was very proud of his three sons and would lie beside their nesting box. When they were just ten days old, with their eyes open for the first time, he threw a squeaky toy into them and couldn't understand why they didn't want to play with him. Minnie was an excellent Mum and never left them for the first four weeks of their life. She adored them and would spend hours licking them all over. They weren't just clean – they were polished.

They grew up to be very successful show dogs. Miguel quickly became a Champion, handled mostly by Tara in the show-ring, Sammy (registered name Pooghans Samuels Skweek) won a Certificate and Marmaduke, the largest of the three, won a dozen Championship first prizes. A couple of years later Minnie and Hector got together again and had another litter of three. This produced Champion Noel, who won an exciting Best of Breed award at the Centenary Crufts and Christmas Cracker, a most adorable dog who nibbles the noses of those he loves, and Holly, who is my special friend. All won well at top shows.

I think Woolly, by now, was a little bewildered at the number of English Toy Terriers that were now being produced. We were too! She played with them all and stole their squeaky toys and they regarded her as a large Aunty. And you know how large Aunties can be! Her circle of four legged friends was now complete. She and Huggy Bear and the odd collection of English Toy Terriers and the cats were all in the house and the Afghans were outside in their kennel and dog run and she could join them whenever she wished. The whole menagerie had different characters and personalities and we didn't have a vicious dog among them.

CHAPTER
THREE

VISITORS

We are very fortunate in having a number of friends and, as a result, we get quite a number of visitors at Buggins Cottage. The place itself is a bit of a novelty to anyone living in the confines of a City. It's a tiny half pint Cottage right on the edge of the Roman Fosse road with a large garden at the back. The dog run and kennels take up a lot of space, of course, and we have a private road to the kennel that is really just a narrow lane.

When we first moved in I inquired at the Council office about buying the road at the side of the cottage and I was told that under an ancient law if I legally had the road closed by a special court in London, the road would revert back to the owners of the land, either side of the road. It sounds complicated but it isn't really. I persuaded the Crown Agents, who owned the other side of the land to sell me three metres of land at the side of the road for £50. That meant I now owned both sides of the road. It cost a few hundred pounds to go to court and legally close the road for the length of my property and then the road became mine.

One side houses the kennels, dog run and the garden. On the three metre strip I planted 22 fruit trees. Apples, pears, cherries and a greengage, and on this land we bury our cats and dogs when they die. We've been at Buggins a long time now and there are dozens of dogs and

25

cats buried there. We have the graves all marked and know exactly where they all are.

It's cold and bleak in winter and more than once we've been cut off from civilisation but the local Council are very good and send a snow plough to dig us out. In the spring and summer it can be delightful. I planted 1200 daffodil bulbs about a year after we moved in and each year they bloom to form a yellow carpet of flowers approaching Buggins. There quickly follows the blossom on the fruit trees – so we have months of colour. Buggins Cottage wouldn't suit everyone but it suits us. It's much more convenient for the dogs than it is for us, but we want to stay there for the rest of our lives.

Most visitors accept the chaotic state we are usually in, with books everywhere and a dining table littered in paper work to do with my radio programmes. There are squeaky toys, the collection grows all the time, and there are files of newspapers and video tapes and prize rosettes and trophies and Championship Show Certificates lying everywhere. The occasional visitor might have their nose in the air but most of our visitors know us well and take us as we are. Woolly, of course, absolutely accepted us for what we were and added to the accumulated mess by bringing in more papers, books and squeaky toys.

Visitors were first treated with suspicion by Woolly but when we welcomed them, so did Woolly. Our first daily visitor was usually the postman who had to go through two gates to get to our back door – or rather, our only door, since we don't have a front or side door. Woolly flew at the postman who always managed to dart to the door, quickly dispose of his letters and escape speedily to the safety of the other side of the gate.

Woolly never actually got hold of him and I'm not sure what she would have done if he had been slower. I suspect she was really after the letters because when they came through the letter box she would collect them and bring them in the house. She did need persuading, sometimes, to let us have them.

When the milkman came, usually mid-morning, Woolly would fly at him but he ignored her – I think he must have had quite a lot of experience with dogs. Woolly never bit him – but she would look 'savage'. She guarded Buggins – her territory – jealously and with enthusiasm.

Living in this isolated cottage on a main road means that anyone who has a car breakdown within a mile of us will come for assistance or to use the telephone to call for help. We kept them outside the gate and put

Woolly away before allowing them in to use the 'phone. I think Woolly might have done terrible things to strangers and I wasn't prepared to risk the consequences – we tried to keep her apart from anyone she didn't know.

We have some good friends in the nearby village of Bingham. The Day family. Martin, Sue, Justin and Melissa, and Woolly looked forward to their visits because Sue nearly always brought her what she called her Woolly bag. There would be bits of meat, biscuit, bacon, cheese – all sorts of tit bits and Woolly enjoyed these enormously. Occasionally some of the other dogs might have a morsel but Woolly didn't really like sharing her Woolly bag with anyone. When Justin once visited us she snapped at him – I think she misunderstood his intentions, and we smacked her hard. We did discipline Woolly if ever she went too far. If discipline was given straight away she would accept it and come to us a few minutes later to say sorry and did we still love her? But if she was disciplined long after a wrongdoing she was puzzled as to why she had been smacked. She didn't get that many smacks.

All our relatives knew and liked Woolly. My daughter, Karen, was a frequent visitor and she didn't really like the English Toy Terriers but she did like Woolly. My son, Digger, pretended not to like the English Toy Terriers but he'd only have to be alone with Hector for a few minutes and I would find them both lying on the floor nose to nose playing games. Digger was very fond of Woolly – she was a real man's dog.

When my brother, Frank, visited us she would sit at his feet and demand attention. He always speaks loudly to the dogs and it worried some of them – but not Woolly. She was a dominant character with other dogs but she didn't mind humans dominating her.

We had two Aunt Ems. One was called Aunt Emily and she lived with us for a while. She pretended not to like the dogs too much, she was a very gentle person and said she didn't like them too near her. One evening we went off to a meeting of some sort and took Woolly with us. When we returned Aunt Emily was furious and when we asked why she said it was because we had left her alone without Woolly. She said she always felt safe when Woolly was with her. I had no idea she felt this way but we made sure that Woolly always stayed with her when she was at Buggins.

Our other Aunt was Aunty Emmy. She was a real character and visited us once or twice from her home in Buckinghamshire. She smoked a pipe – profusely – and Woolly was a bit wary of it. But Aunty Emmy loved dogs and once had a Poodle that 'smoked' and then ate cigarettes. It died a ripe old age so its smoking habits couldn't have done it much harm – though smoking and eating cigarettes is not something I would recommend to two or four legged friends. Aunty Emmy was an eccentric and had been a Music Hall artist and tended to be a little over dramatic with things. She once went into the dog run to see the Afghans and when one of them stuck its nose right up her skirt I apologised profusely. "That's all right" said Aunty Emmy "No one's done that for a long time". She liked Woolly because when she was smoking her pipe and knitting, Woolly would lie down by her side for hours without stirring. Aunty Emmy was an old lady and Woolly must have made her feel very safe and secure.

Woolly lived in her own little den. This lay off the kitchen between the toilet and bathroom. We called it "The Smelly End" – because Woolly did smell a bit. It was all to do with the natural oils in her coat – and other things. If ever Woolly was fed up with the company of other dogs or if she wanted some peace and quiet from the cats and puppies she would lumber back to her den, to the smelly end, and curl up in her basket. She slept there at night and the only problem we would have would be when visitors, who were staying for the night, would knock on our bedroom door, in the middle of the night, to say they couldn't get to the toilet because Woolly was apparently guarding it against all comers. We explained that when going to the toilet – which was only inches from Woolly's den – you had to be bold and march in with determination, showing no fear. Visitors didn't always feel like behaving in this way in the middle of the night – but it was the only way to get to the toilet.

Woolly seemed to know that relatives were rather special and she seemed to identify them even if they were not frequent visitors. Our son, Paul, was a good example. He lived in Wiltshire and whenever he came to see us Woolly would leap at him and make a great fuss of him and his wife, Mary-Jane and their little daughter, Lucy. She did the same to Digger and all our large family. She had a habit that once she accepted visitors as friends she would find an object and bring it to them. It could be anything at hand. A biscuit, a letter, a newspaper, a book, a slipper, a shoe – even a Wellington boot. She'd have it dangling from her mouth, wagging her tail furiously. It was the sign of friendship towards the visitor

Finbar was an exception. She never accepted him. Finbar was a very large Irish Wolfhound owned by some very good friends of ours from near Ashbourne in Derbyshire. Maurice, Sue, Sarah and Matthew Gratian had been friends for many years and whilst we only saw them a couple of times a year the greeting was always warm. Woolly also greeted them all

28

warmly – but distinctly moved apart from Finbar.

One weekend the Gratian family stayed with us and brought Finbar. Woolly made a fuss of them as they came through the door but when she saw Finbar she immediately retreated to the smelly end and stayed there the whole of the week-end and when Finbar came through the kitchen to go outside Woolly raised her head and looked through him as though he wasn't there. I never knew her like that with any other person or dog.

Finbar was a great character and most affectionate. He didn't take any notice of Woolly, which was just as well, and he probably knew it. He had a short tail derived from an argument with a sharply closed door. He got on very well with all the other dogs – though he thought the cats were a bit strange. The cats thought he was strange as well and kept out of his way staying on top of the fridge. Of course if Finbar had wanted to he could easily have reached them on their perch, but he didn't bother. Finbar was all for the easy life. The moment Finbar had gone back home with his family Woolly moved out of her den, had a large stretch and yawn, and came back in the lounge with us as though nothing had happened. I guess if she could have talked she would have kept silent about Finbar.

One day we were visited by Indians.

It was a Saturday afternoon in the height of summer and we were all in the lounge when suddenly the daylight disappeared from the windows. Two huge coaches stopped outside the cottage and an Indian lady stepped out of the coach carrying a young boy who looked as though he was asleep. We went to the door and apparently the boy was an asthma sufferer and needed an inhaler because he had difficulty breathing and he had become unconscious. For some reason we didn't panic though the boy was slumped in his mother's arms. An Indian gentleman then came in carrying a small piece of equipment. He said he needed to plug it into the electricity to give the boy air to breathe. We plugged it in and the boy's mother put a mask over his face and in no time at all he was all right and breathing normally.

We all breathed easier and the Indian lady said it had happened before and there was no need to worry. Then another Indian came into the cottage, then another and another. In no time at all the cottage was full of Indians. There seemed to be hundreds of them all piling into our small cottage. The two coaches probably had over a hundred Indians and they had been to Skegness for the day and were now on their way home to Birmingham. I suddenly thought of Woolly and how she was reacting to this invasion of Indians – all wearing the most beautiful turbans – the men, that is. The ladies were wearing gorgeous Saris. Woolly let them all enter Buggins and they were all very careful to shut the gates behind them.

I must tell you that a few days earlier I had bought a pair of chattering joke teeth. They looked like false teeth, but they were extra large and could be wound up with a clockwork mechanism which made them chatter. Woolly had taken them from us and took them to her den where we salvaged them. I think they were probably on the kitchen table when the Indians first came in. They would be well hidden under food, carrier bags, books, newspapers, letters, bills and bowls of fruit. That's the usual state of our kitchen table. When the cottage was packed with Indians, Woolly made an appearance at the door wearing the chattering teeth like a huge pair of false teeth. It made her look as though she was laughing. The Indians had obviously never seen a dog with false teeth before and began talking – all hundred of them, very excitedly. Woolly, meanwhile, was enjoying the stir and consternation she had created and was now standing full height with her tail wagging furiously grinning her head off with these huge teeth in her mouth. We acted as though all dogs behaved in this way. There was no point in acting in an excited manner. After all, when they brought the young Indian boy into the cottage slumped unconscious in his mother's arms they showed no signs of panic at all. We weren't going to let down the rest of dogdom by acting as though it was away from the norm for Woolly to have a full set of smiling gnashers.

The Indians were obviously worried for our sanity and filed out of Buggins Cottage shaking their heads in disbelief. They thanked us profusely for the electricity supply which saved the life of their young asthmatic offspring and we all lined up outside Buggins waving goodbye to the Indians with Woolly wearing her glistening set of teeth.

I have no idea what was in Woolly's mind when she got the teeth and positioned them in her mouth. I have no idea if she was threatening the Indians, if she was trying to frighten them or, indeed, to welcome them. I suspect she was really laughing at us all.

She did have a way with visitors.

CHAPTER
FOUR

FOOD GLORIOUS FOOD!

The eating habits of dogs can be quite interesting. Like humans, most dogs like a variety of food and they can be choosy as to what they eat. Some seem to manage on very little, others need a lot. Some grow fat on a minuscule consumption of food, others keep thin though they seem to consume a great deal. Over the years we have had some very finicky eaters and we've had dogs with gigantic appetites. Woolly fell into the latter category. She ate and she ate well. As I say, not all dogs are like this. Puppies are a problem sometimes. You aim to get a good quantity of good quality food into them to grow good flesh and muscle and bone. Rather like children. But in a litter of puppies you nearly always get a poor eater who needs special encouragement to finish its meal.

We had a dog called Nipper-Nose. He was a very elegant and handsome black and silver Afghan. He was the brother of Champion Tara and came from Gina's second litter and he was a devil at meal times. He would sniff the food and walk off. He was a fine, houndy type of Afghan, anyway, but he would not gulp his food down like the rest of the dogs. So we had to feed Nipper-Nose by hand. He got his name because he had a long nose with a powerful jaw. His registered name was Zorro of Pooghan and he was a very good show dog and won the trophy for Afghan of the Year.

He sired a lot of very good puppies – but he was never an enthusiastic eater.

Nipper-Nose had a marvellous sense of humour and when something amused him he would throw back his head and open his mouth as though he was laughing. When we fed him by hand, which we had to do until he was well past being a puppy, he would sometimes gently clamp his jaw over our fingers and hold them in his mouth. Now, he had a jaw powerful enough to bite a hand off but he didn't. He would hold a hand in his jaw and look up at us. He tried to look fierce but his furiously wagging tail gave the game away. It was an example of his sense of humour and fun.

Some of the Afghans were very difficult with their food. We have always fed them together because that sometimes encourages the poor feeders to eat, if they think the others are going to gobble everything up and there will be nothing left for them. But sometimes when the food is laid on the ground in a dozen piles, some of the Afghans start to guard three or four piles of food and won't let the others anywhere near. They patrol up and down, growling and nibbling from each pile of food. We never had any serious fights over food and have always been careful to ensure that each dog gets its fair share.

We never had any worries with Woolly. Food was a great joy in her life – any food. She would finish her bowl a long time before the others and she was quite willing to finish off any food left by anyone else. We once had a Poodle called Bumpy, whose other nickname was Hoover, because if ever there were any scraps of food on the floor after a meal, or particularly after a party, she would Hoover the carpet by going round sucking up any morsel she could see. In fact she cleaned up better than any vacuum cleaner. Woolly was the same except she cleared up enthusiastically and often left a crumbly mess on the floor.

Woolly would eat anything. If anyone was eating she would sit nearby looking straight into the eyes of the eater begging for a crumb. I was eating some pickled onions once, they are a favourite of mine. Woolly was sitting upright in front of me and I dropped a pickled onion. She caught it and swallowed it instantly. She gulped and her eyes watered a little but she licked her lips in anticipation of the next pickled onion coming her way.

On Saturdays we like snack lunches, a bowl of soup and ham or pork or garlic sausage with French bread. If we had any visitors they would join in. So would Woolly. She had a habit of picking up a dog bowl and bringing it over to visitors sitting upright in front of them. It was her

begging bowl and inevitably they put food into the bowl. They couldn't resist. The problem was, she knew how to hold the bowl to get food inside but she didn't know how to eat the food and still hold the bowl in her mouth. So, she would drop the bowl, and the food, and hurriedly devour the contents fallen on the floor before any of the other dogs got to it.

Woolly was at her happiest at parties. As soon as the food was on the table she knew somebody would give her something, it was only a question of begging and waiting. She never stole from the table and that's something that the English Toy Terriers specialise in. As unhygienic as it sounds, we would often have a meal with an English Toy Terrier on our lap only to find a piece of meat being slowly dragged off the plate in front of our eyes. Woolly didn't have to do that, she was confident that with a look of starvation in her eyes she was bound to get some food.

It's very bad to feed tit bits to dogs from the table. Very bad. We did it all the time and as a result the dogs came to expect it and they would all be begging round the table. We've had as many as six begging, drooling dogs round the table at one time. It never bothered us but it can be disturbing to visitors to see these obviously starving dogs wanting food. We usually clear the room of dogs if we have visitors, but you couldn't clear Woolly out. She was really the most unsubtle dog we ever had. The English Toy Terriers would curl up in chairs and appear at the vital moment when a fork full of food was lifted to the mouth. Woolly would be there from the time the food was placed on the table. She never curled up when food was on the go. And, as I say, she would eat anything.

We grow a fair amount of fruit in our garden. Not very successfully – in fact we don't grow anything very successfully in the garden but we have fun trying and I find gardening very relaxing at weekends after a hard week's work.

We started a very small strawberry patch and over the years it grew and grew as the strawberry plants trailed at the end of fruiting to root and form more plants. It's always quite exciting to see the strawberries form after the frost has finished. The strawberries are white, first of all, and then they swell and go pink before they rippen into their final strawberry red colour. It's amazing how many strawberries you can get from a fairly small area. At present the strawberry patch measures about 9 feet by 12 feet and recently we picked 60lbs. of strawberries from that patch which began with a dozen plants put into the garden many years ago.

We have a problem with marauders. The occasional rabbit gets into the garden and nibbles anything and everything and we once had a partridge who brought her brood of eight chicks into the garden to attack seedlings. And, if the season is a wet one, slugs come out like an army of hungry mouthed predators – and they are very keen on ripe strawberries.

One late spring when the strawberries were beginning to ripen I went out to see if there were any edible ones because I like taking Marjorie and Tara some very early ripe strawberries for breakfast. I couldn't find any and I was certain I saw some ready the previous evening. I thought it must be the slugs or a rabbit or a pheasant or partridge or any bird easily attracted to the ripe red fruit. That evening there appeared to be more ripening strawberries which would certainly be ready the following morning. Next morning they had gone. During the day I kept an eye on the strawberry patch. Woolly usually stayed with me when I did any gardening but if it was sunny she would lay stretched out on the lawn.

I was in the dog run with the Afghans and saw Woolly get up, shake herself, and saunter down the garden path to the strawberry patch. She was the culprit. She sniffed the strawberries until she found a plump ripe one and ate it. She didn't see me and when I called her she hung her head in shame and dropped a half munched strawberry. I never smacked her for anything like that. As one of the family I guess she was entitled to the strawberries as much as anyone else.

There are 22 fruit trees at the side of the road and when I planted them in the ground each small tree had a bagful of horse manure underneath the root and that seemed to work well because all the trees grew and grew sturdily over the years. The crop of fruit from the trees has been variable. I don't have a programme of spraying for pests because I am rather suspicious about the effect of poisonous sprays on the fruit and anyone who eats the fruit. Sometimes we would get a good crop of apples and pears and plums and cherries but most times we wouldn't.

I knew Woolly was eating the cherries. That is, the few cherries left by the birds that would flock in at the slightest sign of colour on them as they ripened on the trees. The birds would drop the cherries and Woolly would move in. A lot of apples and pears would drop from the trees during the ripening process and there were a lot of half eaten pears and apples left by Woolly on the ground. If she could have climbed trees I am sure she would have gone for the larger fruit at the top of the branches – in fact, she may have done. Woolly could do most things and I wouldn't put it past her talents to climb trees.

We have four Victoria plum trees. Like the other fruit trees they have good and bad seasons. On a bad season you would be lucky to pick a pound of plums from all four trees. On a good season the branches would be bowed down with fruit. There would be an enormous amount of plums and some of the branches would be literally scraping the floor and some branches break with the weight of the plums. Any visitor would be welcome to pick the plums in a good season. There would be far more than we could use.

One year the trees were full of ripe plums and it was great fun picking a juicy plum and eating it freshly picked from the tree. We decided to try and store the plums in huge baskets which we kept in the conservatory. Ripe plums don't store very successfully we found. We suddenly noticed that the basket of plums was dwindling dramatically. There was a basket brimming with plums one moment and it would be half empty the next. It was Woolly, of course. We found her raiding the baskets and eating the plums, discarding the plum stones in the corner of the garden. The same thing happened when we picked the pears and apples. She was taking them and eating them.

I never knew a dog eat so much fruit. Most dogs are not that keen on soft fruit like plums – but Woolly was different from most dogs most of the time. She even started to take gooseberries from the prickly gooseberry bushes in the garden. We learnt it was not 100% safe to leave any food in the conservatory. Most conservatories are spacious and are there to sit in and catch the sun on a pleasant summer day. We treat our conservatory like a storage shed. Marjorie's brother, Ken, bought us a very nice and comfortable three piece wicker set for the conservatory. It consisted of a two seater settee and two chairs. Marjorie made some very attractive cushions for the chairs and settee but Woolly ate them. We tried again with more cushions and Woolly encouraged the English Toy Terriers this time to eat them. So we gave up putting cushions on them.

The conservatory housed dozens of plants, four large book cases, a huge one armed bandit that sometimes worked and a smaller one that didn't. We had a collection of nearly a thousand records in a cabinet, a second-hand set of the Encyclopedia Britannica (1957 edition), a fridge-freezer for food and a small fridge for soft drinks. A vacuum cleaner would usually be stored in the conservatory and there was also a large avocado tree grown from a stone – I'm quite proud of growing that tree. By the side of that was a beautiful camellia bush. You now have an inventory of the contents of our conservatory. It's not very large – just 9 feet by 15 feet, and in addition to everything else we would keep a large sack of potatoes and carrots for easy access.

Woolly liked rummaging about in the conservatory and she would take and munch apples, pears and anything edible. We found her taking potatoes and carrying them to her sleeping basket in her den. She reluctantly allowed us to look into her sleeping quarters. The result even shocked us. We knew Woolly liked carrying things about – that, we thought, was her retrieving instinct. But we weren't prepared for what we found hidden between her blankets and her sleeping basket. There were squeaky toys, half eaten dog biscuits, potatoes and carrots (some chewed). She'd also tucked away a trophy won by the English Toy Terriers, it was a six inch high silver cup. There were also prize rosettes, an empty box of chocolates, dried up flowers that we thought we had disposed of in the garbage bin; there were books, a half bottle of wine, some dog bowls and a quantity of plum stones.

It was amazing that Woolly was able to climb into her bed, let alone sleep with this collection of oddities. We cleared everything out but in no time at all she started collecting items again. I hoard things and am reluctant to clear them out – Woolly was far worse than me.

In the summer we would have barbecues – especially if we had visitors. We have a number of Swedish friends. We started having Swedish girls to help in the kennel in the early days of Riverbank Farm and we have stayed friendly and in contact with them over the years. Inger Hedstrom had been our kennel girl for six months and seemed to enjoy the madness around her and stayed for another six months. She had to be almost deported to return to her native land.

Over the years Inger has visited us many times and recently has brought with her a husband, Urban, and four beautiful daughters, Erica, Sofia, Amanda and little Alexandra. All with different personalities and all great dog lovers. We'd have a barbecue in the garden with the house dogs with us and Woolly would also be in attendance, of course. She would sit upright perilously close to the barbecue fire and if anything dropped on the lawn, it disappeared instantly.

Woolly seemed to have no difficulty with a hot sizzling sausage. It would be swallowed in a gulp. I'm not sure if Woolly ever tasted her food. Woolly liked all the food at a barbecue. That wasn't just hamburgers, chicken pieces, sausages, steak and chops. It included mustard pickle, salad, crisps, pickled onions, gherkins and chutney. Her appetite was as varied as any food available. We'd be sitting round the lawn eating with our plates balanced on our laps and this large Irish Water Spaniel would appear with her head resting on a shoulder snuggling up to our side. The Swedish youngsters would squeal with delight at Woolly's antics. Joyous days.

Woolly liked bread – just bread on its own, it didn't have to be buttered

or have anything on it. Of course if it did have anything on it Woolly liked it even more. She seemed to enjoy stale bread and when there was the odd lump of hardened bread in the bread bin there seemed little point in throwing it away with Woolly on the prowl. She would always take the bread out of the house into the garden. We had visions of her perhaps lying by the hedge near the lawn, chewing and munching at her lump of stale bread enjoying her little feast, away from the other dogs, in her own world of contentment. We found out it wasn't like that at all.

I was digging in the garden one day and I dug up half a loaf of bread, just inches below the surface. It couldn't have been there very long because it was still recognisable as bread. A few yards away I dug up some more bread, and then found more. Over a large patch of garden I dug up about two dozen pieces of bread. Woolly had buried her bread all over the garden. Ours is a large garden and I haven't yet dug every part of it. I mean to, but I have to work for a living, and there's always a patch of ground that gets left each year. I have visions in years to come of digging up bits of bread buried by Woolly years previously. I have no idea why she buried the bread. I know that some dogs bury bones and come back for them a long time after to savour them when they are 'mature'.

Maybe Woolly intended to do that with her stale pieces of bread. She may have been burying bread for years as far as I know. And she had the good sense to smooth over the soil after digging a hole and burying her bread because it certainly wasn't obvious from the look of the garden as to what was buried beneath by Woolly.

The garden was fun, relaxing, but not a great horticultural success – and the dogs didn't help. We have always grown cabbages – with varying success. The Afghan, Huggy Bear used to eat growing cabbages and he introduced Woolly to this tasty delicacy. Sometimes we felt that in the garden we were fighting the elements, nature, and Huggy Bear and Woolly, as well as the occasional rabbit, pheasant, and mother partridge and her family.

I would carefully transplant a row of vegetable seedlings only to find them all dug up and nibbled. I never knew who or what had done the damage – but if there was any taste to the damaged vegetable you could bet Woolly was one of the miscreants. It may have been her excessive enjoyment of food that caused her to grow too tall and overweight. She was inches taller than she should have been and weighed far more than the normal Irish Water Spaniel.

But the word 'normal' was not often used when describing or thinking about Woolly.

CHAPTER
FIVE

NATURAL FUNCTIONS

If you are easily offended I would suggest that you do not read this chapter and move on to the next. If you have never owned a dog you will not know about its natural functions. I do not wish to offend the reader writing about the natural functions of Woolly and her four legged friends so please skip this chapter unless you want to read things that most authors would not write about. You have been warned.

Woolly passed wind – that's really too polite a phrase to use for Woolly. She farted. I know that's vulgar, but she did. And for some time we didn't realise it was her. When you have a number of dogs in the house, as we do, you must expect smells and, as long as they are not too offensive, you have to live with them.

It usually happened in the lounge in front of the fire and when it did it could have been any one of half a dozen dogs. We once heard it but didn't know where it came from, and, for once, Woolly used some subtlety. She got up, moved towards Huggy Bear who was lying in his usual position on an armchair, covering it with legs and body and tail. Woolly growled at him a little. How very clever, we thought, to have identified the culprit and tell us in this way.

Woolly never usually growled at Huggy Bear – he was like everybody's uncle, he never did anything anyone could ever criticise. So Huggy Bear got blamed for the fart. A few days later there was another one and Hector was passing Woolly at the time – she sniffed his back end and growled slightly and we thought again, it couldn't be her – it was Hector.

Woolly seemed to be the only one reacting with these doggy indiscretions and if we'd thought about it that ought to have been suspicious. Woolly got found out because we were in the lounge watching Television and the other dogs were in the garden. There came a loud rip-roaring fart and it could only have been Woolly. She looked round but there was no-one to blame this time. She pretended to be asleep but when we all exclaimed, Woolly!, she got up and came over to us, looking very sheepish, but wagging her tail.

We pretended to be very shocked and she hung her head in shame. It didn't stop her farting. It didn't embarrass us, but it was sometimes embarrassing when we had visitors. Particularly when a Reverend gentleman came to visit us. He wasn't our Vicar but from another Parish where we had a mutual friend. Marjorie went to Church regularly, I'm ashamed to say, I didn't. The Vicar may have called to save me, I'm not sure, but he liked dogs. Hector, unfortunately, had little respect for the cloth and when the Vicar outstretched a friendly hand, he bit him. We evacuated a chair for the Vicar on one of his visits and gave him a coffee and a cake which half a dozen dogs had their eye on. The Vicar was relaxed and asked about the dogs and about us and my work – and Woolly farted. We pretended not to notice, and Woolly farted again – louder this time. The Vicar had perfect manners, of course, and did not mention it. After all it could have been any of the dogs and it isn't really a talking point in nice company, is it? Woolly got up and went out of the room and we breathed a sigh of relief. Minnie, one of the English Toy Terriers leaped on top of the settee and on the way she farted, loudly. It couldn't be ignored and we apologised on Minnie's behalf. The Vicar brushed the apology to one side. "That's perfectly all right" he said.

Woolly had other habits that were natural functions but not nice in polite company. Sometimes she would be out in the garden, come into the house and scrape her bottom along the carpet from the door to the middle of the room. Itchy bottoms must be uncomfortable for dogs and, to be fair to them, they must get relief when and where they can.

I remember once visiting a good friend of ours who lived in the Manchester area. He was a famous Pekingese breeder and exhibitor and he had an exquisite home. We were at a dog show and he won the Best in Show award and we had won the reserve Best in Show. He asked us back to his house for a coffee. We accepted and asked if we could bring a dog. He said he didn't usually have dogs in the house but since our dog was the Afghan, Champion Bonny, and she was very beautiful in her long, platinum blonde coloured coat, and he liked her a lot he said he was sure she would behave herself.

His drawing room had a large grand piano and beautiful furniture and furnishings and a wall to wall white Chinese carpet. I have never seen a floor covering like it. Bonny sniffed the carpet and I wondered what she would do. She did it! She scraped her bottom from one end of the room to the other. We were horrified and we were never again asked back to his house.

We didn't take Woolly into anyone's house unless we were particularly asked to. Woolly drooled a lot and sometimes she looked disgusting with saliva hanging from her jaws. She drooled whenever there was food about – she obviously had no control over herself. She slobbered a lot and since it was an incurable habit we got used to it. It was one of her less endearing traits.

Sexually, Woolly was quite good. When you have a number of dogs and the sexes are mixed you do get used to their sexual habits. Some dogs can control themselves, others cannot. Ours were a mixed lot. When the bitches came into season – usually twice a year when they were ready for mating – we would separate them from the males. Woolly wasn't too much of a problem because Huggy Bear was no longer interested in any sexual activity because of his operation, and the English Toy Terriers were much too small to reach her.

Woolly would be very wicked sometimes with the dogs in the run and go up to the gate sticking her backside through the gate in an enticing manner. It drove the Afghans wild with desire and seemed to amuse Woolly. We once discovered that Hector and Woolly were missing and searched high and low for them thinking the worst. We were sure they hadn't got out of the complex because the gates were all firmly closed – we found the pair of them at the top of the garden. Hector was clinging to Woolly's front leg – he had no sense of direction with Woolly – but there was little chance of him effecting a proper mating. Though you do hear sometimes of a Dachshund making it with an Alsatian – so we were always a little wary with Woolly.

After that Woolly often used to take Hector up the garden path – even when she wasn't in season. I think she liked the attention Hector gave her. And when she came back to the house she would lift the letter box with her nose and rattle it until she was let in. When she first did it we thought it was the postman – and when she did it frequently we would say "It's the postman" but we knew who it was. It was all very puzzling for visitors. She would also knock on the door with her paw.

English Toy Terrier males are sexy little creatures and they all get very frustrated when the females are in season and they are not allowed to be with them. Woolly would relieve their frustrations a little by allowing them to 'ride' one of her legs. We often saw an English Toy Terrier on each of Woolly's legs riding them and dropping off eventually completely satisfied. They also used to ride her ears. As I have said – they had little sense of direction.

Woolly used to have false pregnancies and these could be a nuisance. Around 60 days after being in season Woolly's body would malfunction and she thought she was going to have puppies. She would make a nest in her den and she would even come into milk. Her teats would hang low with milk and she had all the signs of having a litter – but no puppies arrived, of course. At this time she would mother the English Toy Terriers and welcome them into her den area – at other times she would be protecting her collection of odd items in her bed and would growl warningly if any dog approached her den.

The English Toy Terriers learned to keep away from her territory, but when she had a false pregnancy the little dogs were welcome and she would clean them all over with powerful licks paying particular attention to their tummy and private parts. Sometimes the licking was a little too intense and they would squeal and try to move away but she would pull them towards her with her paw and they suffered in silence. I think they quite enjoyed the process and since she was good to them easing their sexual fantasies on her legs they probably felt they owed her something. And sometimes they would queue up outside Woolly's den waiting to be licked. There could be several little dogs forming a line.

At that time we had five English Toy Terriers – Minnie and Hector and their three puppies. Minnie was a very good mother and cared for her puppies until they were fully grown. Her favourite was Miguel, who became a Champion, handled in the show-ring mainly by Tara and occasionally by Marjorie. I never showed the English Toy Terriers. I felt uncomfortable in the ring with them. I had handled the Afghans with great success years before but the little dogs I left to the women-folk.

Minnie, as I say, doted on Miguel and she would wash him every morning after he'd been out in the garden to do his toilet duties. Minnie loved all her puppies but Miguel was special. When Woolly had a false pregnancy and wanted to lick the little dogs Minnie would be quite puzzled and still insisted on cleaning down Miguel after Woolly had finished with him. In turn, Miguel was puzzled by having his second dose of cleaning.

At times of false pregnancies Woolly would collect more squeaky toys than ever in her bed and would 'nurse' them. When she vacated her den Hector would nip in and take some of the toys. He loved playing with them; he'd carry them around with him making them squeak and he'd toss them in the air and catch them. His children would join in and they would have a tug of war with them. One of Hector's favourite pastimes was to toss a squeaky toy downstairs and then rush after it, capture it, and do the whole game all over again.

Minnie was very strange with Hector and his squeaky toys. If he was too exuberant with them she would go up to him and scold him and sometimes take the toy out of his mouth. Hector never answered back to Minnie and would allow her to take the offending toy. It was as though she was telling him that she had a headache and for goodness sake stop all the tomfoolery with toys. But Minnie never chastised her children with the toys and would often join in their games. Woolly would play with the squeaky toys as well but her play was a little rougher.

We decided it would be a good idea if Woolly had a litter of puppies. I am not sure if my theory is correct but I believe it's quite natural for a bitch to have puppies, they are designed for it, they come into season for the purpose and there do seem to be more problems with bitches that never have any puppies. Having said all this the breeding of puppies is quite a serious business and brings a responsibility for those puppies. Big dogs are quite likely to have sizeable litters and a bitch living in a small terrace house can bring chaos with half a dozen or more puppies all over the place.

Puppies quickly grow up and unless you have proper facilities and good homes lined up for them it's best not to plan any litters. Getting the right home is always a problem and a breeder is very fortunate indeed if he or she has no problem in clearing puppies. There are so many horrendous stories of puppies being bought for their novelty value and never settling in properly with a family and going from home to home and ending up being destroyed in a dogs home. I feel so very sad when I hear stories like this. We never easily sold puppies and we had been breeding Afghans since 1962. We asked searching questions of prospective puppy buyers and often refused to sell if we thought we hadn't got the right person for our puppies. We could usually tell on the telephone if someone was right or not – call it instinct.

Prospective Afghan puppy owners had to have a large secure garden with no chance of escape. They had to have the time to spend training the puppy and they had to expect 'accidents' in the house from time to time. Of course, if someone lies when being questioned, there isn't much anyone can do. I think we had a better record than most with our Afghan puppies and I only knew of three occasions where a puppy changed hands after leaving us. One was a very sad incident.

We sold a lovely cuddly playful Afghan puppy to a couple, but it was quite large, and I told them I could not recommend it as a show specimen because it really wasn't elegant enough. They said it didn't matter, they wanted it as a pet, and it would live in the house with their Yorkshire Terrier. We heard no more from them for over a year and they suddenly telephoned us very excitedly and said they'd taken their dog to a show. Warning bells rang in my head and for some reason I was not too pleased. I explained that I remembered when I sold it to them I had said that I didn't think it was a show dog. "But it is" they exclaimed "It's just won five firsts and Best in Show".

I was rather surprised, from what I remembered of the dog, and tried to tell them that it could be a flash in the pan, they might go to a dozen dog shows and never win another first prize – that's dog showing. But they were bitten by the bug and kept showing him and he won the occasional prize. I was concerned, I don't know why, and told Marjorie of my misgivings. They didn't do too well with the dog at larger Championship shows where the competition was much keener. He had turned out exactly as I thought. He was tall, very sound, had a good coat but he was large and had a sizeable head that wasn't really the shape that was desired at that time.

I doubted that I could award a top prize if I had judged him – and I hope I was not as prejudiced as other judges. But how could you tell someone who was so enthusiastic that their dog really wasn't up to top show standard? Somebody did. And that person, who was a prominent breeder, exhibitor and judge, suggested that they should get rid of the dog and buy a proper show specimen. They did just that. They got rid of their delightful loveable dog and bought a dog that had done some winning but was not safe in temperament.

I was furious and made my anger known. The man's wife was very apologetic and said she argued in vain with her husband about getting rid of the dog. She loved it and it had been so friendly with their little Yorkshire Terrier and there had never been any problems. The dog went from home to home and it made me very sad and angry to think that I had sold him strictly as a pet and his only sin was to win 5 firsts and Best in Show at his first dog show.

They won prizes with his replacement but later I learned that it had killed the Yorkshire Terrier and was most unpleasant to live with. I had some puppies for sale about a year later and the man came to me wanting a puppy 'for a friend' – and he didn't care how much it would cost him. I threw him out. That puppy sale of mine always haunts me though I don't think I did anything wrong. And I remembered the incident when we were discussing the possibility of mating Woolly.

Buggins Cottage was ideal for breeding puppies, though we didn't breed many. It wasn't a puppy farm or anything like that. We had a maternity kennel built next door to the dog kitchen and we had a large puppy run in front of that. The garden was extensive and the house dogs had the run of a fairly large lawn area and there was the Afghan dog run. We had all the facilities and we knew all the advertising outlets for puppies and from time to time we had inquiries about Irish Water Spaniel puppies because Woolly's character was known over a wide area.

We were friendly with some Irish Water Spaniel owners in the Lincoln area and discussed Woolly's mating with them. They recommended a dog near Malmesbury, in Wiltshire. It was a full Champion. Gundogs can have two titles – they can become Show Champions if they gain three certificates in the show ring or they can become Field Champions if they gain their certificates with the gun in trials. It really is an achievement to become a full Champion – winning both beauty and working shows.

We had heard about this dog in Wiltshire and saw photographs of him and liked the look of him. People talked glowingly of his temperament and we liked the sound of that too. We were pleased enough with Woolly's temperament at home but she wasn't a show dog. She didn't like strangers approaching her and she wouldn't have stood up in the show-ring. Apart from the fact that she was a good six inches too tall, Woolly wasn't a show specimen. Because of her habit of sitting upright, hard on the floor, she had worn two bald patches either side of her backside that were most noticeable when walking away from you. Her pedigree was a mixture and if you have a bitch like that all you can do is try to improve things by mating with as good a dog as possible.

Malmesbury was a long way from Bingham but if you want to do the best for any breed of dog you should be prepared to travel anywhere, no matter how inconvenient, to get the right dog. Never use the dog next door. That's cheating, unless he is absolutely right in all departments for your bitch. This dog did appear to be right, so we telephoned and made all the arrangements and it was agreed that we would take Woolly to him on a Sunday when she should be ready for mating.

Marjorie and Tara took Woolly and the next few hours were eventful. Mating dogs is one of the most natural functions – it happens all the time – there should be no problems. But there often are. Some owners like the intending mates to go off together and run free and effect the mating when they want to. That method can take days. Some dogs do manage everything on their own – but most need assistance. The rarer breeds don't get too much experience. In some breeds some very fine dogs might only sire one or two litters of puppies in their lives and they might be the top specimens in their breed.

The Champion dog in Wiltshire had sired a litter so he was experienced but there was a physical problem. Woolly was about four or five inches taller than he was. He was the correct size. Woolly wasn't. And even on his tip toes he couldn't manage to reach Woolly. She was keen and started up the garden path with her intended mate, and the dog was keen. But he tired himself out trying to reach Woolly and satisfy himself, Woolly, and us.

Marjorie and Tara arrived at 10.30 a.m. and worked hard for three hours but they could not get the two mated. Woolly was getting frustrated – but, by then, everybody was. And, of course, with so much attention by the humans the dogs were being put off their stride. After all, it must be a bit embarrassing for the dogs when they know they want to do. They know how to do it – and all these humans are around urging them on and holding them and trying to help. Frustrating it is – romantic it isn't. Woolly stood still, at one point, and they put cushions behind her for the dog to stand on. But the dog wasn't used to standing on cushions. They tried to lift him into position but he wasn't used to being lifted up. They tried to get Woolly to squat down a little but Woolly could either stand up or sit down – squatting half way was not in her schedule of actions.

By now the dog was desperate, so was Woolly and everyone else. It was time for a break. The people were very kind and served coffee and biscuits. It was now afternoon and they were all beginning to think that the visit was not going to be fruitful. The owner of the dog took him off for a walk and a swim to cool his ardour. He came back wet through and Woolly took even more interest in him – his wet look stirred her passions even more, it seemed. He tried again but the same problems arose. He missed her by four or five inches. She took him up the garden again and they came back but still nothing doing.

They were all about to give up when suddenly the dog jumped onto a

small wall. Woolly backed up to him, he took a flying leap, and suddenly their love was consummated. Woolly was pleased, the dog was very pleased and the onlookers had to restrain themselves from bursting into applause. Without that wall Woolly may never have known carnal pleasure. They were 'tied' for some considerable time. Woolly intended to make her moment of lustful passion last as long as possible.

It had taken a full six hours of hard work on the part of everyone. The stud fee was paid – the dog had certainly earned it – and Woolly returned home with Marjorie and Tara with a look of gleeful pleasure on her face. She had proven to everyone that she was all woman.

CHAPTER *SIX*

LOVE AND AFFECTION

Woolly soon showed signs of being pregnant and this time it obviously wasn't a false pregnancy because with two or three weeks to go her tummy was bloated and the puppies could be clearly seen as she lay in front of the fire. She had an uneventful pregnancy apart from eating more. We gave her vitamin and mineral supplements which some dogs don't like at all. Needless to say, Woolly enjoyed the tablets and powders. We kept a special eye on her when her time was near because puppies can come three or four days before or after the expected date with no problem.

One morning we heard little squeaks from her bed. Three puppies had arrived in the night. No fuss, no bother, Woolly had not needed any assistance she'd just got on with the job herself. Six more arrived before mid-day, and that was it. Nine puppies, six boys and three girls.

She was a very good mother and loved her puppies dearly. She was a little rough with them but they could take it. From the very beginning they were strong and sturdy and there were no problems. You don't see too much of puppies first of all and the mother is usually very protective, particularly if any strangers come anywhere near. At ten days the pups opened their eyes – and then tragedy. We came in from a shopping expedition to find that Woolly had lain on one of the puppies and suffocated it. That's pretty rare but it does happen at times. We took the puppy away and Woolly didn't seem to be at all concerned. She had another eight to take care of and love.

At about 3 weeks the puppies started to crawl about and Woolly kept an eye on them. They didn't stray too far from her. They grew quickly and at 6-8 weeks they would follow Woolly in the garden and would sometimes spend time in the puppy run with her. Woolly's puppies were born quite some time before the English Toy Terriers arrived on the scene so they had the run of the house almost to themselves. She had a good milk supply and was still feeding them at ten weeks and by then they could take food from a bowl. They were weaned at about 3-4 weeks and when they left any food in their dish, Woolly would clear it all up.

Since they were water spaniels we gave them watery names like Water Polo, Water Cress, Water Lily, and Water Fall, and so on. We advertised them because we decided to sell them all – we felt that Woolly was enough Irish Water Spaniel for the kennel. The response to the advertising wasn't very good. Advertising in the local paper did not produce many inquiries because very few people know what an Irish Water Spaniel looks like. We advertised in the Leicestershire area and that drew a slightly better response since it is known as a gundog County.

Three or four puppies went into Leicestershire and we were stuck with the rest. Woolly, by now, had grown disinterested though she still played with them and cleaned them by licking hard when she felt they needed it. We put the last three puppies in the large kennel with the Afghans to see if they would mix. In the run they were all right and the Afghans accepted these rather strange looking dogs. They slept together at night but we had trouble in the mornings when all the dogs were let out of the kennel into the dog run. The Irish Water Spaniels came out first and then guarded the doorway and wouldn't let the Afghans into the run. There was the danger of fighting and we didn't want this to develop so we brought them down into the maternity kennel which housed them with plenty of space and they had the large puppy run in the daytime.

We advertised again and reduced the price, which I didn't like doing. We have never over charged for our puppies but have asked a fair price, the theory being that if someone pays a fair price for a pup they will care for it better than if they get it for nothing. That theory doesn't always work in practice but, basically, it is a fairly sound way of selling puppies. We cleared the rest of the Irish Water Spaniels and we asked a lot of questions of prospective buyers. We refused a couple of callers who were obviously not suitable and I think overall we got good homes for all the puppies and many of the owners kept in touch with us for sometime after.

I know that one did quite well in the show-ring and it seemed to us that all of Woolly's puppies were better than she was with breed points. And one of the things about breeding is that you should always try to improve your stock all the time. Woolly wasn't the slightest bit upset about her puppies leaving but she had proved to be a good mother, she loved them and cared for them while she had to. You can't ask more than that.

I have always been interested in the behaviour of dogs and particularly with the development of temperament with an eye on affection and the way this is demonstrated. Dogs show their affection in many different ways. We have an English Toy Terrier called Christmas Cracker – he was born a few days before Christmas – he is **very** affectionate and likes jumping on top of a box and throwing himself in your arms. He then nibbles your nose. Whilst this is not common with all English Toy Terriers, one or two of ours do it – but not with the passion and fervour of Christmas Cracker. He also responds very emotionally to the mention of his name. You only have to whisper "Cracker" and he trembles with emotion. Hector very occasionally nibbles noses and he also has a habit of pressing his nose against your face and when he does this you know he loves you.

The Afghans were somewhat different since they are naturally dignified and aloof – but not all of them are that way inclined. The bitches were sometimes very demonstrative. Champion Zaza was particularly friendly with everyone and with the immediate family she was quite passionate with her kissing. You only had to cuddle against her head and a huge lick would swipe you across the face. Zaza was very well behaved and lived in the house and only occasionally went into the dog run with the rest of the dogs. We always explained to the dogs when they began their show career that if they became Champions they would live in the house and at one time we had three Champion Afghans. When Marjorie and I got married the three Champions attended the wedding and caused quite a stir in the street outside the Registry office.

As I say, dogs demonstrate their affection in different ways. We have an Afghan called Teddy Bear who leaps into your arms – and I really mean leaps. If you're not prepared for the onslaught Teddy can knock you over. He also has a habit of looking right into your eyes at close range and giving a lick on the face. Ashley is another Afghan who demands attention first thing in the morning. He's been with me on Television a couple of times including a film I made about Afghan racing. He was pretty disastrous at that and only ran a few yards and then tried to remove his muzzle. This Television film was so popular it was used by most Independent stations in this country and on Satellite Television abroad. We have an Afghan called Princess who "speaks". She's very distant and rarely gives kisses but sits bolt upright in the dog run and when she's spoken to in a certain way she will toss her head back and makes all sorts of noises, a little howl, a gurgle, a slight bark. She really does "speak" and once demonstrated this on Television. I had told my TV bosses about the talking Afghan and they risked it live on Television, which was very bold. But Princess came up with a great performance and talked and talked and talked.

Our Champion English Toy Terrier, Miguel, also speaks – or rather, he says one word – "Arf". I have no idea what it means but he says it usually when I come home from work. As soon as I arrive at Buggins he prances up and down puts his bottom in the air and his two front feet low to the ground, tosses back his head and says "Arf". He only seems to do it for me but it's a signal that he wants to be picked up and cuddled. Now the strange thing is that as soon as I pick him up he goes all distant and dignified. He's kissed Marjorie and Tara but he's never kissed me. But when I sit on the settee to have a meal – the table is always too full of things to use – Miguel comes and tucks himself into my side and will stay there for hours with his head in my hand.

Champion Tara, the Afghan, was very strange with her affection. She really was a clown with a great sense of humour. She enjoyed making people laugh and this extended to the show-ring. We went to a Championship show in Scotland once and there was a well known judge who was small in stature. When I moved Tara up and down for him I knew she was going to do something but I didn't expect what she did. She was looking at me and laughing and that was a signal that some mischief was afoot. She looked at this small judge as she moved towards him and suddenly slipped her lead and leaped over his head and landed on the table behind him. He didn't hesitate and gave her the Certificate. Later a fellow exhibitor came up to me in a furious state and said she was going to report Tara to the Kennel Club for unfairly influencing the judge. I said if she did I would support her because there was no doubt that Tara had influenced the judge!

Tara was strange with visitors. My mother came very regularly both to Riverbank Farm and Buggins Cottage when we moved there. Nanny was registered blind and had very little sight and she was once sitting on the settee with Champion Tara who was sitting facing her bolt upright. I had been in the kennels cleaning out and came in to hear Nanny talking to Tara. Nanny said to me – "Who is your friend?" I told her it was Tara. "The dog?" queried Nanny – "But I was talking to her and I could see her nodding at what I was saying".

Tara had a habit of ignoring people usually who sat on the settee and she would sit with her back to them. But if she was ignored she would turn round and poke them in the ribs with her paw. I was very proud of breeding Champion Tara and she was immensely popular with everyone and she is mentioned with affection in a number of dog books.

Champion Zaza's son, Sultan, was a very good companion and pal. He was a big masculine dog and once he was past puppyhood he stopped kissing but his tail was never still and he loved us a great deal. He wasn't too keen on showing at dog shows but he did well and won a reserve Certificate. I remember taking him to Crufts once and he showed well and won a good placing but in the ring he looked at me as though to say "I only do this for you, Dad". Going out of the ring an old breeder called me over and said "That dog talked to you, didn't he?" I had to admit that he did.

Sultan was the pack leader and was a strong disciplinarian with all the dogs in the kennel. If anyone stepped out of line he would see to them. He was a very good leader and had a good influence on the temperament of the dogs. When we had puppies we used to introduce them to the other dogs in the run as soon as possible and usually the adult dogs took to them well. But Sultan used to growl if they came anywhere near him. He wasn't nasty, he was just telling everybody who was boss. At least, he behaved in this way when we were looking. But one day I looked into the run and Sultan didn't see me. There were two or three baby puppies about 5 or 6 weeks old in the run and Sultan was playing with them.

He was very large and they were very small and he was putting his paw out to them, kissing them, and he let them swing on his long ears. It was one of the most delightful scenes I ever saw in the dog run. Then he saw me and changed dramatically and growled at the puppies who sped off to their mother for protection.

Once, at Crufts, Marjorie was approached by the Daily Mail who were doing a feature on the show. They asked about our dogs and took a lovely colour photograph of Tara with four of the English Toy Terriers and published it in the Mail on Sunday. One quote from Marjorie published in the paper was very true. She said whenever we get home we get attacked with love by all the dogs. And that really puts it in a nutshell.

Woolly came into this very friendly environment which really didn't encourage anything on four legs to have a bad temper. She was a character all on her own and was very deeply affectionate with all the family and friends and visitors she knew well. Once a visitor was accepted by Woolly they would get the full loving treatment. And if they brought her a tit-bit well, that was the way to her heart

We had a Swedish friend of long standing, her name was Kristina Husberg and I worked with her co-editing a book called Leo C Wilson on Dogs. Leo C Wilson was a distinguished dog judge. Kristina was a distinguished judge, as well, and was puzzled at first that we should have Woolly, who was certainly not a show dog. When Kristina knew Woolly's character she soon realised why she was so important to us.

Whilst she was still a young puppy Woolly made a Television appearance. I was interviewing a Vet about Parvo Virus, a disease which had just struck the streets of the Midlands in a dramatic way. The point we were trying to make was that this killer disease was a great risk to all dogs and could wipe out rare breeds unless action was taken with a protective inoculation. Woolly sat on my lap during the interview and we used her to illustrate the danger of an unprotected puppy. The Television appearance was very effective. The next day there were queues outside almost every Veterinary surgery in the Midlands and I was told that the Television interview earned thousands of pounds for the Vets locally.

Woolly behaved very well for most of the interview and sat on my lap where the camera got some good pictures of her with her funny curly top-knot. But the bright hot lights got to her in the end and she slumped down to go to sleep with her nose very close to my clipped-on microphone. Her heavy breathing was picked up by the microphone and the interview ended with her snoring gently into the homes of a million viewers in the Midlands.

Woolly wagged her tail a lot. So did all our other dogs but Woolly's tail was thick and she hit everything in sight with it. A dog's tail can be very sensitive, if you step on it the dog will very soon let you know. But the word sensitive was inappropriate for Woolly and she would smack her tail against the furniture and never blink an eyelid. If her tail ever hurt her with its exuberant wagging she never showed any pain. She always wanted to be loved, particularly by the family. If my brother Frank came to us with his family she would sit by his side for hours just to be touched by him. And my sons, Digger and Paul, always played with Woolly and she loved their attention.

For her, full contentment was sitting on the settee with me. After a hard day's work I would flop on the settee, have my meal, turn on the Television and fall asleep. Woolly would climb on the settee, gently, for her, removing any other dog there might be in her way and lie fully stretched beside me with her head on my lap. And she would be there for the rest of the evening. If she didn't come to me I would call her and she would get up, walk from her den, push open the door and walk in. She was heavy and would sometimes try to sit on my lap. But she wasn't a lap dog really – she was twenty times bigger than the English Toy Terriers.

She enjoyed a bath – and always needed one. The Irish Water Spaniel has a naturally oily coat which has a smell. She liked rolling in the dirt in the garden – especially on a warm day. So, when it was time for a bath she would happily leap into the large pot sink in the dog kitchen to have soapy foam all over her and have a good rinse and brisk towelling. Jubilee Jim, a black Poodle lived in the dog kitchen. He was one of the most amiable dogs we ever had and he had a habit of welcoming Woolly into the dog kitchen for her baths.

Most of the dogs weren't too keen on baths and had a look of great suffering during the process. Some of the Afghan dogs didn't mind because on the rare occasions they were used for stud work they were always bathed beforehand and I think some of them thought a bath always preceded nuptials.

After her bath Woolly would make for the garden, if it was a warm day, and roll on the lawn. She was so heavy we never needed a roller on the lawn, Woolly did the job very effectively. Sometimes she would go into the house and roll on any material, towels, coats, blankets or the settee. Woolly did most things with great enthusiasm and drying herself after a bath was no exception.

She loved wearing things. There were the false teeth and she would happily go about with a pair of spectacles if anyone put them on her nose. At Christmas time she would raid the Christmas tree and take a silver garland from it to wear round her neck. She was amused by our reaction.

We had a Poodle a long time ago called Dunri who loved wearing necklaces and would proudly walk about with a string of pearls around her neck. When she died we buried with her a box of chocolates – her favourites – and a necklace. Woolly wasn't devoted to wearing a necklace in the same way but when she felt like it she would wear things round her neck – she liked wearing dog collars. She was friendly at one time with one of the house Afghans called Zenobia, a lovely silver Afghan, but the friendship ended when Zenobia chewed Woolly's favourite collar which was lying on the floor. Woolly was furious and hardly had anything to do with Zenobia again. She really bought back her introduction.

A friend of ours, Bob Coles, had a video camera and often called in to take videos of all the dogs. Woolly was his favourite and we have some excellent videos of her with the other dogs playing about in the garden. Bob was fond of dogs and once owned an affectionate Poodle. If ever he sat down on the settee it wouldn't be too long before he was surrounded by English Toy Terriers, the odd Afghan and Woolly. Woolly would snuggle up to him and push her head underneath his arm. And she would bring him the odd gift of anything lying around, a slipper, a glove, a book or a flower she'd taken from the garden.

Most dogs like affection and respond. Woolly craved it and if ever I kissed her she would always retaliate with energetic kisses. She loved us to be in the garden with her. We had two hammocks. One was slung between two apple trees and various members of the family would lie in it. Tara used to like to do her home work lying in the hammock. Woolly would try and climb in too, but it really wasn't large enough for two, and she would have to be content lying nearby on the lawn. She liked lying in the sun but if it got too hot she would go and lie on a swinging hammock seat which was in the garden. Nanny liked sitting on this hammock and Woolly would often lie beside her as a companion and guard.

Nanny was always a little worried about dogs sleeping together. "Won't they have puppies?" she'd ask. It was difficult to explain to Nanny that dogs can only have puppies a couple of times a year when they are ready for mating. Nanny belonged to an era when these things weren't discussed in the open. Nanny particularly liked cats and when she came to live with us she was rarely without a cat on her lap. Nanny was quite frail and she was a little concerned when Woolly clambered on her armchair to look closely into her face. But Woolly knew her own strength and took care with Nanny.

She was also very careful with my grand-children and when Digger brought his wife, Sue, and Genevieve and Tristan, Woolly would always treat the children with great care. If they were lying on the floor she would tread carefully around them. If Tristan was eating his rusks Woolly would sit directly in front of him, drooling, and Tristan would give her one and howled with laughter when Woolly took it from his fingers. Woolly was a messy eater and when given a biscuit would break it up and leave crumbs everywhere. The English Toy Terriers cleaned up after her.

Woolly was capable of great affection but when she was told off she was also capable of sulking and going off into her den. But it would not be long before she was back again putting her head on to someone's hand for a tickle. She was usually the first to say "Sorry!" after any naughty behaviour. She didn't hold grudges for long. I think she knew life was too short for that.

CHAPTER
SEVEN

HATS AND COATS

One of the great delights for our dogs has been going for walks. When we want to take them out we don't call "Walkies!" or anything like that. We say, fairly loudly, "Hats and Coats!" and then, usually, pandemonium breaks loose. "Hats and Coats!" means we put on their collars and leads and the phrase causes a great deal of excitement. At Buggins we have our own private road or lane which is a quarter of a mile long. It's used sometimes as a footpath by people walking from the village to the bus stop on the Fosse Road and we have never objected to this because it is important that our dogs get used to seeing people occasionally.

Our road has a grassy overgrown verge either side, full of good smells for a dog. And, nearby, we know we have two barn owls, foxes, kestrels, many different types of birds, including a charming yellow wagtail which comes to us every year. We also have stoats, weasels and I think there's a badger about the place somewhere. There are also field rats, voles, mice and families of partridges and pheasants. They all probably cross our lane at sometime or other and you can imagine the scents they must leave behind. Small wonder the dogs enjoy their walks.

Some of the dogs run free and are very obedient and come back instantly when called, but some of them have to remain on a lead because we are never quite sure whether they would run off on to the main road which is always menacingly near.

Woolly was always able to run free on the lane. We did take a lead for her in case someone came along the lane on the way to the bus stop or if anyone came on a cycle. She would rush up to them and roar, rather than bark, and it could really scare them. And if ever she saw the postman on his cycle she would have knocked him over to get at his letters. If anyone came in sight we would put her on a lead to restrain her, otherwise she was free to sniff the sides of the lane or the hedgerows.

It was great having Woolly run free because that was something we could never do with the Afghans. They were always unreliable when we took them for a walk and they always had to be on a lead and under tight control. Mind you, with their long dog run, the Afghans always got plenty of exercise. Woolly loved her walks and, next to food, they were her main source of pleasure. We would take the dogs for a walk in batches of three or four and give them all a turn each. But Woolly had to go every time so she often got several walks a day. And you couldn't leave her behind. She would sit at the gate and look as miserable as sin until we opened the gate and let her on the lane.

She would sometimes cower at the gate in a way that looked as though we beat her every day. She was a great ham actor in the way that she behaved when we were taking the dogs for a walk. Visitors would say "You don't hit Woolly do you?" as she cowered down looking as though we beat her up regularly.

Over the years we have had a lot of kennel assistants and the first thing they have wanted to do is to take the dogs for a walk. That simple function is one of the more pleasant sides of kennel work, believe it or not. There are plenty of sordid things to do with a large kennel of dogs.

At Riverbank Farm two little sisters from the village used to come in and help occasionally with the Afghans and Poodles and they would take them for a walk on the river bank at the back of the farmhouse. Diane and Shelley were not very large at the time but they used to come at weekends. They are both now grown up with families and we see them now and again. We had quite a number of Swedish kennel girls who came over on an au-pair basis. They would stay for three or six months usually, except Inger, who stayed for a year and then came back again. And we see Inger and her husband, Urban, and their children once every two years when they come and stay for a couple of weeks.

Inger was very good with the dogs and she had to put up with a lot because when she first came to us I had very little money. We could safely

64

leave the kennel in her hands and visit relatives some distance away. One day we returned from such a visit to find Inger in tears. A man had called to re-possess the gas stove because I had fallen behind with payments. She was so upset. But we all clubbed together and bought a second hand gas stove to replace the one removed.

When Inger reluctantly returned to Sweden she recommended several other Swedish girls and there followed Siv, Silva, Cina, Annette, Lonnie, Lena and Merika. As a result of these Swedish contacts I was always happy to go to Sweden to judge at Championship shows and I would meet most of the girls again on my visits. Sweden is a long way away and these days the only contact with them all, apart from Inger, is a Christmas card.

We had a kennel boy at Riverbank Farm called Billy who came from Reigate in Surrey. By the time Billy came along I was earning some money with my BBC work, but not much in the early days. Billy brought with him his Border Collie named Beatles, and she was a very obedient dog – very different from the Afghans. Beatles' best trick was to close doors whenever anyone ever came into the room. I thought that was very clever at the time because the Afghans didn't do any tricks at all.

Nanny came once or twice a week to Riverbank Farm and she would take the dogs for a walk usually with a kennel girl. Nanny's favourite wasn't a dog – though she loved them all. Her favourite was a small goat called Fiona. She asked to take the goat for a walk when we first got her and since Fiona would happily walk on a dog lead there was no problem. It wasn't until Nanny had taken Fiona for a walk half a dozen times that we discovered that she didn't know she was a goat and thought she was a new dog we'd bought. She did think it strange that Fiona stopped to eat hedges and grass all the time. And Fiona did eat anything and everything. The branches of trees, anything growing in hedgerows, garden flowers, bushes, shrubs. Her appetite probably prepared us for Woolly who came along some years later. Fiona lived quite happily in the dog run with all the Afghans, a Smooth Haired Fox Terrier we were looking after, and Daisy, the small Dexter cow that we had as a pet at the time.

At Buggins we had a number of kennel girls and one boy, David, who was really earning a bit of pocket money at weekends with us prior to joining the R.A.F. David was very tall – he seemed over six feet, and he wasn't really a doggy person, but he was efficient and the dogs liked him. Among the girls who worked at weekends we had Carol and Jo, who both lived in nearby villages. They worked hard in the kennel, cleaning and scrubbing and feeding and preparing the dog food. They all enjoyed taking the dogs for a walk and they were always safe and reliable.

We were approached by an employment agency to see if we could take on someone for some work experience full time for six months, and that's how Karen came to us. She worked with enthusiasm – in fact Karen did everything enthusiastically and sometimes the dogs wondered what had hit them. She was enthusiastic about cleaning out and feeding and walking. She loved the dogs demonstrably and sometimes when the house dogs would much prefer to snuggle up to the Rayburn stove in the kitchen they would run in all directions to avoid her when she had to bath them or exercise them. Karen left us to go to another kennel which was much more disciplined and organised than ours. She was dreadfully unhappy and came back to us after her painful experience there. We still see Karen who visits us now with her husband, David, and their young son, Anthony. Woolly got on well with Karen because, just as Karen would do things with enthusiasm, so did Woolly.

It was great taking Woolly for walks and sometimes we would go in the fields with her where, once again, she would be free to roam but would always come back when we called. In the fields her nose would be stuck to the ground, there were so many smells and holes to explore.

Woolly didn't like anything unexpected. Hector, the English Toy Terrier, would love to inspect anything unusual but Woolly was wary of anything strange. We once came across a tractor parked in a field and she wouldn't go round it. She stopped in her tracks as though it was some prehistoric beast from a million years ago. No amount of coaxing would make her move and we had to put her lead on and drag her past, protesting all the time.

Woolly barked, of course, like any other dog, but she could also imitate the howl of the Afghans and she did this very effectively. So much so that we very often dashed outside in the garden because we thought an Afghan was loose only to find it was Woolly with her head thrown back and howling, like a hound.

And Woolly roared. I don't know where she got this habit from but it certainly scared any unexpected visitor. To have a big dog roar at you when you're not even sure what breed of dog it is was, to say the least, disconcerting. Frankly, we quite encouraged Woolly to do this to complete strangers. When we first moved into Buggins we were told by a friendly policeman that almost certainly we would be done over by villains who would probably break into the house and steal anything inside. We were warned about tramps and there was the problem of motorists who had broken down on the Fosse Road.

Buggins is very isolated, there isn't another dwelling in sight and it was quite comforting to have a guard dog like Woolly capable of roaring. And, believe me, she could make a blood curdling roaring sound which came from deep within her. A complete contrast to the English Toy Terriers who would only yelp and bark.

Woolly enjoyed travelling in the car – I think. Living in the countryside, one of our pleasures is to go out for a run in the car on a summer evening – maybe ending up in a pub. We would set off not knowing which direction we would turn, even at the bottom of our lane, and then we would go wherever the car was pointing. On such journeys we would nearly always take a number of dogs – Afghans, English Toy Terriers and always Woolly – unless we left her to look after Aunt Emily.

Woolly would demand to go into the car and she would put on the cowering "please don't beat me" act at the gate. She would happily leap into the car. In fact, Woolly would happily leap into any car with an open door and was a continual embarrassment if we took her into Nottingham. If she passed by a car with an open door she would leap in and took some persuasion to get out. She usually had to be dragged out.

So – you have the picture – of Woolly demanding to get into the car. But once she was in she did occasionally curl up on the back seat, but mostly she was restless and would start whining. She wanted to be in the car with us but would still whine and cry, even with a car full of passengers and dogs. We would open a window to let air in and she would stick her nose out of the window, snorting away furiously. She liked the wind in her face blowing her hair about.

She loved going to pubs and would demand her own packet of crisps and eat them with us. She also liked pork scratchings from pubs and any other pub grub. The other dogs would feed from what she dropped and she was messy with her food. We would always get the question at pubs: "What is it?" We'd explain that Woolly was an Irish Water Spaniel and they would go off muttering "Never seen anything like that before". Well, Woolly, was unique! If there was ever a guess at what she was they'd ask "Is it a Poodle gone wrong?" Woolly mostly ignored everyone else at pubs though she was often the centre of attention. She would sit by us and eat as many crisps as we could carry to her.

On long journeys in the car there was more chance that she would settle down and she loved going places. With a large kennel of dogs to look after and take care of we have, for years, been restricted with our travels. The kennel assistants were able to look after the dogs without too many worries but we never liked to be away too long. Nowadays with slightly fewer dogs we don't have any regular kennel help and it is difficult to get away at all. But when Woolly was with us we would take her off visiting relatives.

Marjorie and Tara took her a couple of times to our son Paul's place. Paul and his wife Mary-Jane and their daughter Lucy lived first of all in a charming cottage at Lambourn in Berkshire. Paul worked as an assistant trainer in a famous horse racing stable. Paul and his family then moved to Wantage in Oxfordshire, into a large farmhouse which had great character. Woolly thoroughly enjoyed herself there. There was a stream running through the garden and on the water there were always half a dozen ducks, including some Muscovvy ducks. There was also a pony called Brandy and a couple of Jack Russell dogs called Present and Piggy.

Woolly totally ignored the dogs – it was as though they weren't there. And she wasn't interested in the ducks or Brandy. But she was interested in the water. She went in and didn't want to come out. The stream wasn't deep enough for her to swim but she enjoyed paddling. The stream was connected to a large pond in which there were trout and where the ducks swam. Woolly was respectful of the ducks and didn't go into the pond as though that was their territory. She loved the stream and it's perhaps a bit sad that with all her inborn love of water – after all she was an Irish Water Spaniel – we didn't have any water at Buggins for her to enjoy. The River Trent is over a mile away at Gunthorpe but it's a busy stretch of water with speed boats and water skiers and rowing boats and canoes. Woolly wouldn't have liked all that activity. Woolly was very happy at Paul's place. Unfortunately it was some distance away otherwise I think she would have been a regular visitor.

We took her to Mablethorpe, on the East Coast, a couple of times. I bought a caravan on a site at Mablethorpe, quite near to the beach. I had envied friends with caravans by the seaside and liked the way they seemed to relax at their mobile holiday homes. I paid £150 for the caravan and since I was too busy to see what I had bought I sent Karen, my daughter, and her mother to look it over. I bought the caravan from a man who had been out of work for some time. He asked £50 for it but I gave him an extra £100 because I felt sorry for him and I didn't like the idea of owning a caravan worth only £50.

The caravan itself was a bargain, it was cosy, had four berths, a sink, a stove and a fireplace and lots of crockery and cutlery. But it was disastrous from the point of view of value. I had visions of travelling the 80 miles to Mablethorpe every week – end and staying at the caravan. In fact in the three or four years we owned it we made two half day visits and we worked hard painting it on the outside on both these occasions.

On the first visit I reported to the lady who owned the site and told her I was the new owner and she informed me that the rent hadn't been paid for the past two years. I accepted some responsibility though I had only owned the caravan for a few weeks. She asked me to make her an offer on the overdue rent. I didn't know what to say and was just about to offer £25 when she said – "How about £250?" I numbly gave her a cheque and vowed to get value out of the situation. But I never did.

On the two visits to the caravan we took Woolly, of course, and Nicky, the Poodle. They loved it and were both let free to explore the site. They stayed near the caravan while we painted it furiously. After the first coat of paint we went on the beach and Woolly ran free. She made for the sea and we had visions of her swimming across to the Continent but she came back when we called. There was a cafe on the beach and the smell of food drew her to the large wooden hut in which it was situated. She enjoyed her lunch of sandwiches, meat pies and crisps.

I was sorry we didn't visit the seaside more often because Woolly loved it so much and was very good with the children who came up to her. There was a little incident at Mablethorpe, I remember. To get from the beach to our caravan meant crossing a couple of roads with little traffic on them but for safety's sake we put a lead on Woolly. She wasn't used to the lead because we didn't use it that much and I was running with her when I slipped and fell my full length. I was winded for a second or two and scraped my knee on the road gravel and tore my trousers. I let go of the lead but Woolly came straight back to me and stayed with me until I was able to get up, quite a bit shaken.

She was upset because I think she felt responsible for me falling over. When I was on the ground she came up to me and nudged me with her head as if to see I was all right. And she licked me and loved me. I was very touched.

We never took Woolly to any big dog shows. We knew she wasn't a show specimen and we knew that she wouldn't like strange Judges opening her mouth to look at her teeth and feeling along her bones and body. We took her to a couple of Exemption dog shows. These are very informal shows where the intention really is to have fun. Wins don't count for much at these smaller shows and there are classes for pedigree dogs and cross-breeds and you get classes for "The Dog with the Waggiest Tail" and "The Dog which looks like its Owner".

Our Afghan, Ashley, won reserve best in show at one of these

Exemption shows and won a couple of rosettes. Woolly took one of the rosettes and ate it – much to the disgust of Ashley who had worked hard to win it. I think it was his first show.

Paul organised a small horse show once and had an agility course for dogs as part of the novelty section of the show. Woolly thought the horses were very strange – she wasn't very familiar with horses. Digger took his Border Collie, Flo, into the agility course and Paul took Woolly. There were a number of obstacles to jump over and it was all very energetic. Woolly did her best but she liked to do things in her own way and in her own time and didn't take too kindly to being under control all the time on the agility course. But she won the second prize and beat Flo. She was very proud of the rosette she won and when we got home she took it into her den and never slept without it.

The Afghans, Poodles and English Toy Terriers won, literally, thousands of prizes and cards and rosettes and Certificates, Groups and Best in Show awards – and, at last, she was a prize winner with a second prize rosette to prove it.

CHAPTER
EIGHT

THE END

We often found ourselves talking to Woolly as though she was human rather than a dog. I can remember when she would climb on the settee to lay full length by my side. Most evenings I would say to her – "What would I do without you, Woolly?" It never really crossed my mind that there would come a time when Woolly wasn't there. She was so much part of the family and part of the furniture and fittings at Buggins Cottage. It was unthinkable that one day we would be without her. But the day had to come and it happened dramatically and unexpectedly.

It is difficult for me to write this. Woolly was so full of life and lived her life to the full but it is only right that I should write about her end – her final chapter. Woolly was always in rude health – that's an apt phrase for Woolly. I don't think she ever went to the vets for anything apart from her inoculations. I've asked everyone and no-one can remember Woolly having a day's illness. She could eat anything and nothing would upset her. She was very sturdily built and was not affected by cold or anything. So it was rather strange one day when Marjorie put her food dish down and she rushed to it, as usual, but didn't eat. I didn't think too much about it at the time although it was unusual for Woolly, most dogs have their off days with food and you tend to think "they'll eat when they're hungry". She did the same thing several times that day – rushed towards the food but didn't eat it as though there was something wrong with the taste.

The following day again she rushed for the food but didn't eat.

We examined her and Marjorie took her temperature which was normal. The glands in her neck appeared to be swollen and she had some small nodules down her front and in her chest that bothered us. We couldn't think what it was and went to the dog books but there was no description of her symptoms. I got hold of the Afghan book I had written many years earlier and which had a fairly comprehensive chapter on illness symptoms but there was nothing there and we were very puzzled.

Meanwhile Woolly was fairly normal in her behaviour, she was active, cheerful, funny, loving – all the usual Woolly characteristics. After three days without food she was starting to lose a bit of weight and obviously something was wrong, so Marjorie took her to the Vet. I wasn't really too concerned because I'd seen many dogs in much poorer health than Woolly appeared to be, and they recovered, with no ill effects. Marjorie came back with Woolly and said – "She's not going to make it". I asked her what she meant and she said that after a thorough examination the Vet was sure that Woolly had leukaemia and she would only live another few weeks.

I was angry and told Marjorie I thought the Vet was totally wrong and ridiculous. The glands on her neck probably meant she had a touch of tonsilitis. Woolly wasn't ill – she had some symptoms but she wasn't ill. I said we would have another opinion. But we didn't take another opinion. The glands on her neck grew larger and you could feel nodules down to her chest and on the back of her back legs. And she rarely ate any food though she still rushed to her dish as though she was going to take it all down in one gulp.

She was never in pain and I checked with the Vet about this – he asked to be kept in touch though there was nothing he could do. We had some tablets for her and they seemed to work and for a week she was back to her normal self. I think they were to encourage her to eat, but she never really ate a full meal again. The two things she eagerly did was to walk and eat. She stopped eating but did carry on with her daily walks until one day when she set out with Marjorie and Tara and a whole gaggle of little dogs to go down the lane. She only made it half way and collapsed. Marjorie went to her – she was exhausted. That was the beginning of the end. We were very upset although in many ways she did try to carry on as normal. She was able to play with the dogs a little and she would still roam about the garden. But she was lying down a lot and almost any activity exhausted her. She was still able to climb on the settee for a cuddle for a couple of hours and she seemed to want to be close to us more than usual.

I was still hoping for some miracle and I couldn't come to terms with her illness. I know someone who lives with Leukaemia and has a normal life and appears to be clear of symptoms. I thought maybe that would happen to Woolly.

I didn't even dare think of putting her to sleep. I have always been reluctant to do that with any dog. We owned a great number of dogs over the years and only twice have I had a dog put to sleep. One was Ranee, a very affectionate and dainty black and tan Afghan who went to a skeleton with her illness and couldn't walk without falling down all the time. It was only fair to put her to sleep. And there was Iggy Pig, a beautiful golden Afghan, who was a big show winner for us. He started to lose the use of his back legs and we couldn't improve his condition. One day Marjorie came to me in tears and said we had to put him to sleep because he couldn't walk any more and the insides of his back legs were raw where he had tiddled and wet himself. That was a very sad day because Iggy Pig was a great dog and had a beautiful loving nature. But he was in pain and, I guess, the two things to influence me to put a dog to sleep would be them having constant pain that couldn't be relieved by the Vet and completely losing the use of their back legs. Woolly was getting this way, I knew it, but I couldn't bring myself to think of it – yet.

On the morning of Wednesday, May 30th 1990, I let the dogs out as usual and Woolly slowly followed the English Toy Terriers into the garden. I let the Afghans out into their run and brought down their buckets of water to clean them and fill with fresh water and I passed Woolly who was lying on the lawn, looking very tired. I stroked her as I went past and she lifted her head with some difficulty. I filled the buckets and put them in the dog run and cleaned out the kennel and came back to Woolly.

I'll never forget the way she looked at me. She lay there and her tail gently moved as I knelt beside her. She tried to kiss me but it was an effort for her. She snuggled her head against my hand. I went into the cottage and said to Marjorie – "I think Woolly's dying. I'm going to stay with her". I telephoned the Day family and told them if they wanted to see Woolly they'd better come quick. I went to Woolly. She got up and I thought for a second she was all right, but she collapsed after a few hesitant steps. She was looking at me and I knew she was asking me to do **something**. It was then I thought I would have to have her put to sleep. I put an arm round her and that seemed to comfort her. I knew it wouldn't be long and I just hoped the end would be peaceful.

I started to think about her life. The little puppy that had come into our lives some ten years before and the way she had played ball with me and brought the ball back to my feet for more play. I thought of all the journeys we had made together – the fun she had at the caravan at Mablethorpe. I thought of the false teeth and the invasion of Indians, and the way she brought her begging bowl for food. I thought of her roar, her sense of humour, the fun we'd had. I thought of her puppies and the care she'd taken of them. Of her friendship with all the other dogs in the house and the kennel. Of the way she had guarded and loved us for ten years.

Sue, Martin, Justin and Melissa arrived and came over to where Woolly lay in my arms. She saw them, lifted her head – she may have wondered if they had brought her a Woolly bag of tit-bits – but there was none this time. She wagged her tail a little and then died in my arms.

Her family were all round her, Marjorie and Tara and me and her friends, the Day family. And it was all over. No-one spoke, we were all full of tears. Marjorie brought out a blanket and covered her over. Thank God the ending had been fairly peaceful – distressing for us – but peaceful for Woolly, which was the main thing.

Martin dug a grave for Woolly just in front of one of the pear trees and we buried her with the same ritual as all the other dogs. The grave is fairly deep, there is a bedding of straw at the bottom. She is wrapped in a blanket and then another layer of straw is above her. We put her favourite leather collar and a small box of chocolates and her rubber ball alongside her.

The Afghans in the dog run were all lined up along their fencing on the other side of the road watching us. They had seen the ritual many times before.

As I write this there are 47 cats and dogs buried on the side of the road between the fruit trees. Woolly is buried between Starr and Popcorn. Starr was very beautiful, a deep red colour. Popcorn was a light golden colour and was always tossing her head back and laughing at us.

I asked some members of the family and some friends for their comments about Woolly. This is what they said.

MARJORIE: According to the book an Irish Water Spaniel is one of the most intelligent dogs. Woolly never read the book. She was big, clumsy, undainty, unsubtle, a crazy dog who just wanted to be with you and love you. A walking garbage disposal. She meant well!

TARA: Woolly was smelly; Woolly was funny; Woolly was lovely. She was unforgettable with her gutsy roar and the two bald patches on her bum. Her beauty was unmatchable. This is probably all over the top – just like Woolly.

DIGGER: When visiting Buggins now the first thing you notice is the noise of the traffic. This was not so when Woolly was there. The decibels of her barking always drowned out any surrounding noise. This was soon forgiven with the smile she gave us. And to remind everyone she was around, a swift whip of her tail was all that was needed.

KAREN: I remember Woolly as a big, cuddly old softie. A very loveable and affectionate character, full of bounce, protecting her den but always with an ever wagging tail.

PAUL: What hit me first about her was her smell, she carried it around with her wherever she went and it wasn't in short supply, I liked her a lot. I adored her and wanted one of her puppies but I wasn't in a position to have one when she had them.

SUE: On first meeting Woolly her piercing eyes un-nerved me but she soon became my best canine friend, winning me over with her cunning little ways. Sneakily drinking my coffee and crafty attention-seeking nudges. Kitchen scraps became an expected "Woolly bag". I loved Woolly!

INGER: She really was a clown – her most appreciated antic was the false teeth trick when she would dash around grinning like a lunatic enjoying the attention she got from us all.

BOB: Woolly, I would say, was a very special friend. Now that she has gone, to sit at Buggins without a wet nose pushing against your hand for a bit of fuss, seems very strange. And I miss her a lot. Buggins will never quite be the same.

These are comments from some that knew Woolly.

No, Buggins isn't the same without Woolly, but when you mourn the passing of someone very special you also think about all the things they did that made you love them. And that's what we think about Woolly now. Never a day passes without me thinking about her. When there's coffee over in the jug you think that Woolly would have liked that. If there are scraps of food on a plate you think – Woolly would have enjoyed that.

Her roar is gone – but it is remembered. Woolly's gone – but, in a way, she's still with us. I pass her grave at least a couple of times a day and I know that she is at rest. If there is a Heaven for dogs she'll be there, bossing everybody. And she'll be with a lot of friends she knew at Buggins.

We never had a bad dog or cat that would go to any other place than Heaven.

And in the spring I know the pear tree will be heavy with its pale blossom which will eventually fall, covering Woolly's last resting place with a blanket of delicate colour.

I can still see Woolly's gamut of expressions. Quizzical, knowing, laughing, loving. I can still see her waddling up the garden path, wagging her tail.

I feel she is by my side as I write this. I hope she is nodding in approval. I don't think she'll be surprised by our declared affection. She knew she was loved.

And there's no way that she will ever let us forget her.